HOCKNEY
ON PHOTOGRAPHY

HOCKNEY
ON PHOTOGRAPHY

Conversations with Paul Joyce

Harmony Books / New York

For Joan, Wendy,
Nathan and Sammy

Published by Harmony Books, a division of Crown Publishers, Inc.,
225 Park Avenue South, New York, New York 10003

First published in Great Britain by Jonathan Cape Ltd.

HARMONY and colophon are trademarks of Crown Publishers, Inc.

Manufactured in Spain

Library of Congress Cataloging-in-Publication Data 88-24691

ISBN 0-517-57174-9
10 9 8 7 6 5 4 3 2 1

First United States Edition

Contents

Paul Joyce made these interviews over a period of 4 years, the same period I was experimenting with a camera.

He simply kept turning up, and as our friendship grew I was at times eager to talk (as I listen to myself) on other occasions I was too intensly involved in what I thought was complicated construction and therefore uneager to talk. Nevertheless he persisted in his endeavour and here it is.

For myself, "Pearblossom Highway" finished the intense period of photographic work. My photographer friends said it wasn't really photography but painting. I'm not so sure, but I think thats where I'd like to leave it.

David Hockney

Los Angeles May 2nd 1988.

Introduction

One afternoon towards the end of June in 1982 I walked into London's Knoedler Gallery in Cork Street to cast an eye tired by countless unmemorable photographic images over what I expected to be an exhibition of old Hockney snapshots. I emerged blinking into the sunlight. This was one of those rare moments in life when a fundamental change of vision occurs.

I came to photography relatively late in life, in my mid-thirties, after some years as a film, theatre and television director. Because I had a trained eye, I was able to achieve results very quickly. Within two years of serious photographic experimentation, I'd had a one-man show at the National Portrait Gallery in London, received grants from the Arts Council of Great Britain and the Welsh Arts Council, shown my work extensively in Europe and North America, and was putting together my first book. To all intents and purposes I'd arrived. Then I stopped taking photographs. There was something unsatisfactory about the medium. I did not know what, but it had frozen me in my tracks.

This book is many things, but one motive at the beginning was an attempt to answer the misgivings and doubts which had led to my personal 'photographic paralysis'. David Hockney took me on a journey of discovery, or rather led me beyond the bounds of ordinary consciousness into a land where anything is possible. The text that follows charts this voyage.

During the five years that he and I were talking, Hockney's photographic work was widely published. He has always said that if you show people another way, they will follow. The fact is that I was the only person connected with photography to pursue him in search of new insights about the medium. Most professional photographers chose to dismiss the work as merely provocative or playful, and the ideas as contentious or irrelevant. Some took the superficial aspects and appropriated them for their own purposes without understanding their real depth and power. Even respected critics have tried to explain Hockney's massive photographic outpouring as a kind of theatrical gesture, and by implication some quirk or flaw in an otherwise serious artist. This strikes me as a basic misreading of the ideas behind the work. I hope this book will lay such misconceptions to rest.

All the work on display at the Knoedler Gallery in 1982, and the thousands of photographic pieces Hockney has made since, have at their core one revolutionary ingredient: a moving consciousness at war with established notions of photographic 'realism'. Once that rigid barrier was smashed, Hockney was free to reconstruct the world as he sees it, and not as any single camera lens might interpret it. This was the essence of the revelation which struck me five years ago. No other photographer has ever managed to place himself firmly within the world under scrutiny with the compassion, humour and precision of Hockney.

Perhaps one needs to have practised as a photographer to understand how restrictive a single lens can be, at least when it is producing a single image. It has nothing to do with whether the format is 120, 35mm, 10 × 8 or even panoramic, nor does it hinge on the number or focal length of one's available lenses. All these relate to technology, never to a *way of seeing*. When Hockney picked up his little Pentax 120, the question furthest from his thoughts was quality of image. He was more concerned with speed, mobility and silence (the Pentax has an electronic shutter, and is virtually noiseless). This pocket camera helped him make some of his most memorable 'joiners'* – although it was a camera which any professional would disdain as a mere toy (in fact Hockney stuck a Mickey Mouse transfer on his Pentax, so people would think just this). This may help to explain the degree and strength of professional resistance to Hockney's ideas and techniques. He has little time for received opinion, which

---

* Joiner – Hockney's word for a large composite photograph.

9

by definition is locked into the past. He is a visionary in the land of the frozen one-eyes.

As soon as I got home that summer evening in 1982 I wrote to Hockney, a stranger out of the blue. He called me next day, saying that he knew *someone* would respond to his work. He was apparently eager to talk. A couple of days later I loaded my Morris Minor with cameras and tripods (for my 'photographic paralysis' had undergone a miracle cure) and drove to Pembroke Studios. This was the beginning of our five-year-long conversation. The whole morning disappeared. The phone was simply left to ring, other people with appointments sat around waiting, nothing could interrupt the flow of ideas. Hockney said he had thought about these things so intensely and deeply that he felt at times he was going mad. Not mad, I replied, you're going sane! During those three hours I saw a man radiating more energy than any artist I had ever met. I could imagine that when harnessed to his art such energy could be frightening. Indeed, he told me that Christopher Isherwood, when sitting for a photographic joiner portrait, had likened him to a mad scientist.

It was soon clear, during that first session, that Hockney had been wrestling with conceptual problems presented by the photographic image for a very long time. He had been shooting pictures consistently for over twenty years, pasting the resulting chemist's prints into countless large albums, and tossing the negatives into old cases. A selection of his early work had already formed the basis for an exhibition at the Centre Georges Pompidou (Beaubourg) in Paris and for a book.* A glance at that book revealed that he was experimenting with multiple images and 'cut-ups' in the early 1970s. But it was not until he discovered the Polaroid SX-70 camera and film that he was able to put all the preparation time to such stunning effect. The square format of the Polaroid image allowed him to arrange the individual shots in combinations both vertical and horizontal. Thus he was able to build up a formalized and rigorous grid allowing him to extend pictures as far as he wished to.

As Hockney will explain in this text, the 'trigger' for his

---

* *David Hockney Photographs* (Petersburg Press, 1982).

first Polaroid joiners was his inheritance of some unexposed packs of film; he simply picked up a camera and began to experiment. But it's clear that this apparent accident would have happened sooner or later. For his early work was never tentative; it appeared in a sense fully formed, to the point that Hockney himself was taken by surprise. He would get up in the middle of the night to study the joiners in progress, looking at them excitedly but with an objective eye, almost as if they had been done by someone else. The intensity of his daily work, combined with the sessions at night where he looked and learned, led to a massive concentration of effort and hundreds of new pieces.

For the first few months of photographing (approximately February–July 1982) Hockney's medium was predominantly Polaroid film and the results are different in character from the later photocollages. Apart from the special colour quality of the Polaroid stock (due in part to the technical process whereby the development of the image takes place *within* the film sheet itself), all the Polaroid joiners were mounted with an equal white border around each image. By the time Hockney had picked up a conventional 35mm reflex camera he was ready to experiment with direct mounting without borders, so that the work became *collage*. He found this change from Polaroid to 35mm (and the smaller 120 format) both liberating and convenient. Films could be processed at the one-hour 'Fotomat' down the road and the shooting process could be executed much faster. He did not have to wait two to three minutes for each individual Polaroid to develop. But the main change was that when Hockney used 35mm he had to keep the whole picture *in his head*. The Polaroid process allowed for a gradual build-up of images and permitted quite a measure of second thoughts and changes to the original concept over the three to six hours each work took to produce. Using conventional methods the picture remained firmly in his head and in the camera until the films were processed, so he had to narrow the margin for error. This extraordinary discipline combined with freedom from the Polaroid camera led to an explosion of creative activity lasting not months but years.

The range of subject matter and the physical size of the

works he showed me that morning at Pembroke Studios demonstrated just how exciting and deeply engaging he found this process to be. I remember thinking that by overturning the established parameters of photography, he might just end up photographing the whole world.

At the end of our conversation, well after lunch time had come and gone, I remembered the Pentax 120 I had slipped into my pocket before the visit. I'd acquired this after seeing one of David's photographs of the gardens at Glyndebourne* where the early-morning mist and the actual grain of the film combine in the print to create an ethereal, magical world. He smiled at my request for a single portrait, particularly after the nature and content of our conversation, but happily stood in front of an unfinished (and since abandoned) oil portrait of Ian [Falconer]. Looking at the oil now, one can see that the photographic experimentation was already beginning to feed back into his other work. And surely this is one of the keys to his productivity. Each medium in some way complements the other. Far from being a detour from his principal work, as many critics originally considered them to be, the photographic pieces have acquired such authority and strength that they now unquestionably occupy a central position in Hockney's development.

The following conversations were recorded mainly on a pocket machine in locations which changed almost as frequently as the topics under discussion. Sometimes a session would merely clarify points raised previously, and these have been incorporated (I hope judiciously) into the body of the text. Occasional repetitions have been eliminated, but it was clear as the informal interviews progressed that Hockney constantly goes back in his mind to things which have been preoccupying him. Usually when he returned to a topic he did so with new insights, and the text reflects this organic process.

It is rare to be allowed to share the thought processes and working life of a great artist. The demands on Hockney's time are phenomenal, and when he needs to he simply cuts himself off. That he never did so with me says as much, I think, about his belief in the importance of our conversations as about the relationship which developed between us. I was lucky and persistent enough to be there at the right moments. Hockney says that art can change people's lives. I always hoped and believed that this was true. This book stands in praise of that belief.

---

* 'Glyndebourne, Sussex, 1980'.

London, 1988   PAUL JOYCE

11

Pembroke Studios, London: July 1982

PJ: You've always used photography as an adjunct to your painting, as a tool. But was there a time when you suddenly realized that your photographs had some real quality of their own?

DH: I had been taking photographs for years, and if I do anything, I do it seriously. I have thousands and thousands of photographs, and they're all stuck in albums, just like anybody else's. I never edited them. I just stuck every one in. I always went to the chemist to have them processed, mostly as colour prints. I don't take photographs in the way that a professional photographer might do, taking, say, sixty of the same thing. I didn't file the negatives. They were just chucked in a box, but I did keep them.

When you look at my albums you can see by 1971 how much better the pictures get. They are much more carefully taken. They are more considered. I was standing still then and groping very slowly. You do gradually see an eye at work, and a sensibility, but that took time. With a lot of the early

photographs, I just pointed and I thought: the camera is only seeing what you see. But if you don't see anything in the first place, you can't photograph it. When I found that out it made me more interested, and I realized that some of the photographs I'd intended to use for paintings didn't have to become paintings.

There was a point in the paintings when it looked as if I was becoming obsessed with verisimilitude, which I know is not interesting painting. It can be technically interesting, but great painting is not like that. And as I moved away in painting, I became conscious that a photograph was another thing completely. Some of them were strong enough as images to exist on their own. And so I did become more interested in the photograph as the photograph.

I'd still never shown any, partly because nobody had asked! Picture dealers such as Kasmin* had never shown any interest

---

* John Kasmin, known as 'Kas', long-time friend of Hockney's and his dealer since the early 1960s.

Mr and Mrs Ossie Clark (photograph 1970)

Mr and Mrs Clark and Percy (painting 1970–1)

Myself and Peter Schlesinger, Paris, December 1969
(two-piece composite photograph)

in my photographs, so I never bothered. Then in 1976 Ileana Sonnabend* published a portfolio of mine in Paris, called 'Twenty Photographic Pictures'. Each photograph sold for three or four hundred dollars, which I thought was *quite* enough. Later the price went up, and I thought: this is crazy, to pay all this money for photographs; you can just print some more, after all, you've got the negatives. I couldn't understand it. If you make an etching, you have a limited edition. You just can't print that many: the plate would fall apart. There's a good reason for printing only a hundred or so, but photography isn't like this.

It all began in earnest when Alain Sayag from the Beaubourg in Paris came to choose some of my photographs for an exhibition there in 1982. He had seen the portfolio, and was interested, not because I was a photographer, but because I was a painter who took photographs. But he had no idea that I'd taken so many! I said: you make the choice, there are too many. And I meant it because I didn't want my time taken up. I was busy trying to paint again, since I'd just finished in the theatre. So he stayed for a week. Every day he would go through the photographs, and every night we had long arguments about photography. I would say how boring it all was, how photography could never be as interesting as drawing or painting.

I noticed that his eventual choice of photographs tended to be quite formal. In the show in Paris, even in the book, the amount of pictures within pictures, frames within frames, is very large. Not many of my photographs are actually like that, but he emphasized that aspect in his selection. I couldn't find all the negatives for him, so at the end of the week he dashed out and bought some Polaroid film to copy the prints of the albums. The day after he went home I realized he'd left a lot of unexposed film lying around. I thought: I can go mad with this!

PJ: What, specifically, started you off on the joiner photographs?

DH: I didn't plan the joiners, they just happened. There was a

---

* Ileana Sonnabend, art collector and publisher.

Gregory, Pembroke Studios, London, 1977 (colour photograph)

Study for Portrait of an Artist, Le Nid-du-Duc, 1972 (colour photograph)

period in the late sixties when photographers were using wide-angle lenses a lot, and the photographs were awful: everything was distorted in a way that you never see. That was what put me off – you just *never* see in this way. I knew there was something deeply wrong with it. I thought I'd rather just join the pictures together: even if they don't fit, it's more interesting, more honest, and it gives you a feeling of space. If I'd used a wide-angle lens to photograph this giant room, for instance [Pembroke Studios], I don't think you would achieve the same feeling at all. Of course, I was working blind, trying to remember the previous picture I had taken and where it had ended, and so on.

Shortly before Sayag had arrived I'd done a painting of the living room in Los Angeles. Both the living room and the terrace were combined into one picture. When he left, I just re-did it on Polaroid film, and glued it together. That was the first one! I pinned it to the wall, and I kept going back to it. Even in the middle of the night! It was different, somehow. It was a narrative, a story, you moved, the viewer's body moved through the house. But the main point was that you read it differently. It wasn't just a photograph. It was abstracted, stylized: the ideas were based on cubism in the way that it filters things down to an essence. It was just eighteen pictures – nine, in two rows – and it worked so well that I couldn't believe what was happening when I looked at it. I saw all these different spaces, and I thought: my God! I've never seen *anything* like this in photography.

Then I was at the camera night and day. Within a week I'd done very complex things. I went and bought a thousand dollars of Polaroid film straight away! I quickly discovered that you didn't have to match things up at all. In fact, you couldn't possibly match them, and it wasn't necessary. The joiners were much closer to the way that we actually look at things, closer to the truth of experience. And within a week they had developed amazingly. I then began on that huge one of a group of people.* It took about two hours to do, and when I'd finished I nearly collapsed. I was astounded because I knew it was alive, and normally a group photograph is the most static of all.

At that point I realized it was more than just a novelty. I decided to stop painting for a while to pursue the joiners and just stop when I got bored. The problem was that I didn't get bored: it got more and more fascinating. And it got harder as I pushed it, and became even more interesting to me. I had to do a lot of calculations in my head and the amount of concentration needed was enormous. I couldn't break off; I ignored everybody else. I just forgot about them because I was so involved. Christopher Isherwood thought I was like a mad scientist!

I had begun a painting, twenty foot long by seven foot of Santa Monica Boulevard.† I used to walk up and down it, and the main problem was that it was seen from one point of view, essentially. I had struggled at that painting for six months, trying to make it look as though you were walking

---

* 'Steve Cohen, Ian, Gary, Lindsay, Doug, Anthony, Ken, Los Angeles, March 8th 1982' (see page 20).

† 'Santa Monica Boulevard, Los Angeles 1978/80'. Abandoned for no particular reason.

My House, Montcalm Avenue, Los Angeles,
Friday, February 26th 1982 (Polaroid collage)

Schwimhalle   Munchen

972.

U.H.

Schwimhalle, München 1972
(composite photograph)

along. But when I started the joiners, I realized I could now paint the Santa Monica Boulevard picture *another* way. They told me how to do it.

PJ: It occurs to me that the one element you say is missing from photography is that of time. But even joining up three pictures, taken almost simultaneously, injects . . .

DH: Time. Yes; I realized that very quickly. It seemed that these pictures had added a new dimension to photography. I had wanted to put time into the photograph more obviously than just in the evidence that my hand pressed the shutter, and there it was, it could be done.

The big joiners of Kasmin, Spender and so on took about four hours to do. Consequently there are four hours of

Kasmin Smoking, 27th March 1982
(Polaroid collage)

layered time locked in there. I've never seen an ordinary photograph with four hours of layered time. That's *much* longer than you would take to look at it! This is what it's overcome. For me the main problem in photography always came down to that. Any drawing or painting contains time because you know it took time to do. You know it wasn't made with a glance: if it's honest work you know it must be a genuine scrutiny of the experience of looking.

In the exhibition [Knoedler Gallery, June 1982] each photograph is quite different, or it is to me. Some are very spatial and others are not. The one I did of David [Graves]* is spatial because I was going way, way behind him and taking pictures. I remember realizing how much I was walking about. The space was much bigger than the room.

PJ: You must have left your subject there for half an hour!

DH: Oh yes. He thought I was crazy, taking a photograph of him when I was way over there photographing some plant!

There are aspects of the joiners that I don't fully understand, probably because I don't know enough about optics. Somebody said I should use a better camera, but the only one that was suggested produced rectangular pictures, not square. I thought the joiners had to be square because then they would work in a diagonal way as well. You can't help but relate each square to eight other squares, therefore there must be a permutation of numbers you can look at.

One extraordinary thing I discovered was that you can go on and on looking at these pictures, which is very unusual with photographs. However good the photograph, it doesn't haunt you in the way that a painting can. A good painting has real ambiguities which you never get to grips with, and that's what is so tantalizing. You keep looking back. A single-eyed photograph can't have that quality: when you look back, it's the same. But even though I'd made those joiners I still kept looking at them days later. Once you start looking, you're drawn into them, and you cannot not look unless you turn away. There is a movement going on which keeps changing. It's a very complicated process: It's not just a number of

---

* David Graves, assistant to Hockney 1980–7.

David Graves, Pembroke Studios, London, Tuesday 27th April 1982
(Polaroid collage)

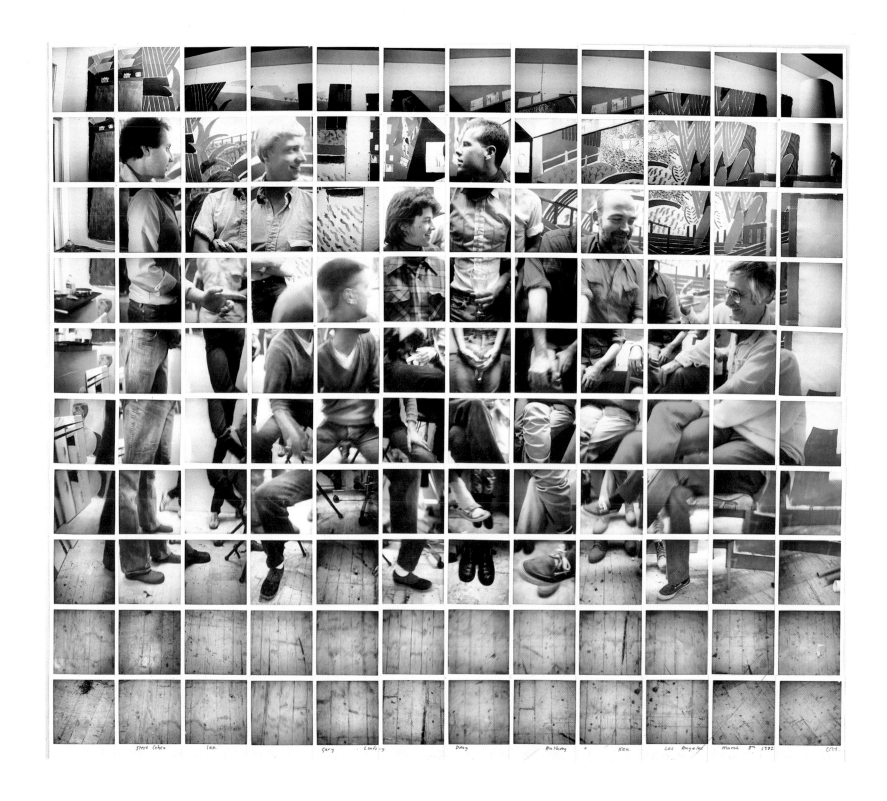

Steve Cohen, Ian, Gary, Lindsay, Doug, Anthony, Ken.
Los Angeles, March 8th 1982
(Polaroid collage)

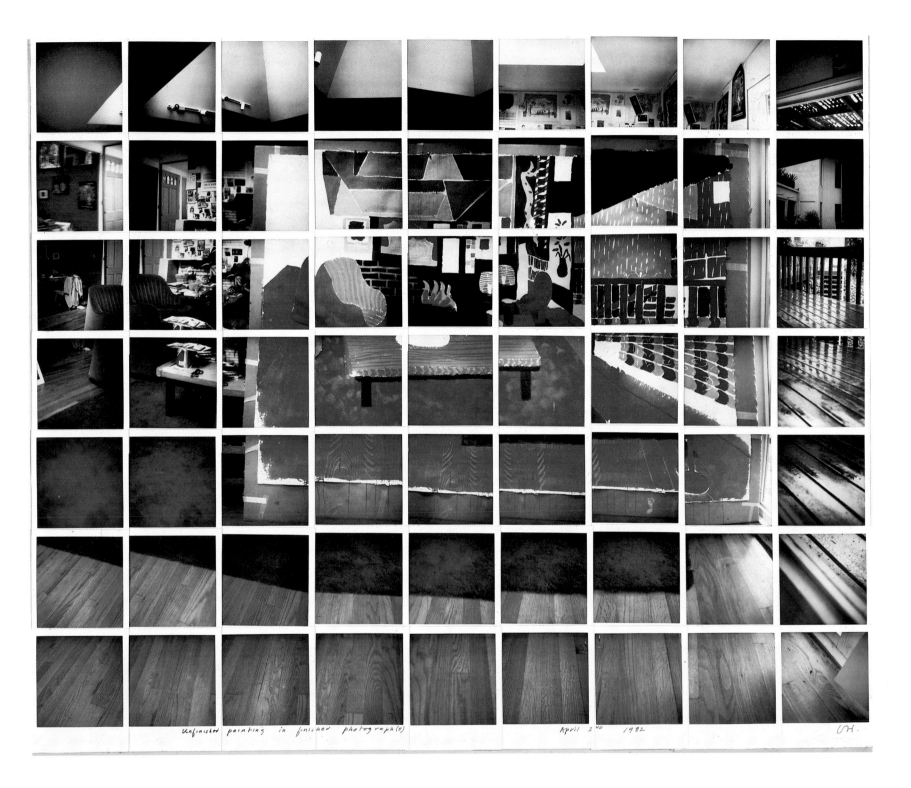

Unfinished Painting in Finished
Photograph(s), April 2nd 1982
(Polaroid collage)

photographs you look at. The combinations of pictures have much greater possibilities than that. To me this represents a complete reversal of the usual qualities of photography.

After three whole weeks working on the joiners I could hardly sleep: I used to get up in the middle of the night and sit and look at them to find out what I was doing. Everybody who came to see me was equally excited, so I knew it was working. After all, they usually wonder what I'm going on about! So I just went on and on, and finally the burst of energy that had lasted about three months wore out. That's a long time. Every artist gets bursts of energy in an inspiration, but they don't usually last that long.

At the previous show in New York one or two critics were impressed just with the amount of work. They knew I had been working for nearly three months, but all they were looking at was a third of my output during that time, and they didn't know it! The first reaction was from an art critic, who thought it was interesting, but just a novelty. A week later a photographic critic who I didn't know [Andy Grunberg] wrote about it and he was much more interesting, he'd looked harder, and being a photographer he would have known about the thinking process involved.

From the moment the New York show opened they had a lot of people visiting. Just people who went out and said to others: you *must* go and see them.

European-style Dark Tent, wood engraving, 1877

PJ: That's how I came to see the show. Wendy [Brown] came back and said: you've got to see that, it's the most interesting thing that's happened in photography for years. So we got straight in the car. And I must have told half a dozen people, key people . . .

DH: . . . who would believe your word.

PJ: Absolutely. How often are you *really* excited about something? But maybe there is some quality about the joiners which even you haven't come to terms with.

DH: Yes. Naturally I got excited enough to try and analyse things, as you do when you stop and sit down. And I figured out a great deal because I do know a bit about the theories of cubism. For instance, in Western art, the camera has dominated *looking* for three hundred and fifty years at least. So the camera is a lot older than photography. The camera obscura was discovered about 1580, and it was a camera even though it was just a room with a hole through which the scene was projected. Canaletto, Vermeer, many artists used one, and, naturally, they were fascinated by what was happening.

It occurred to me that in Western art things always stop at the top, bottom and sides. With the invention of the camera obscura, easel-painting really flourished. The idea of painting before was always on much bigger areas, such as walls or ceilings, and so the edges were far away: painting was not about edges. But with this idea of the window, the camera leads inevitably to an interest in verisimilitude. By the nineteenth century a lot of artists realized there was something wrong with this. It was not quite truthful.

And in European art certain artists started to escape when they noticed Oriental art, and Japanese art in particular, which is based on Chinese art. Of course, the Japanese and Chinese did not have the camera until the nineteenth century. I have to assume they didn't because it's not in the art, there's no evidence of it being a one-eyed art. But when you think of the Renaissance, those artists were always looking with one eye, looking through a hole. Oriental artists had different ideas. They could depict a landscape as a *scroll* which you open out. Then Manet and Van Gogh saw some Japanese prints which must have looked unbelievable to them in the

22

Camera Obscura,
wood engraving, *c.* 1840

nineteenth century. Marvellous and simple. Here was an art that dealt with essences, not with verisimilitude which is about surfaces. So they were fascinated and it influenced them. Manet's forms became simpler and bolder. They accused Manet of being like a child, which is just what they called Picasso. We can't see it now.

But the bigger break comes with cubism – it's an unfortunate name and it wasn't given for any real reasons. Essentially, it's a different way of looking, and it's about reality and perception. In the art world cubism has been greatly misinterpreted as being about abstraction, which it's not. The late theorizers of cubism never say it's about abstraction, they know it's about perceiving the physical – how we see; what we see. What the cubists did *was* difficult to see but any intelligent person instantly responded to it. Within ten years it had enormous influence, and within twenty years it had influenced everything – showing a way to do things more simply. However obscure it was in the beginning, whether there was a mass audience was not the point. It had reached just enough people to filter the ideas down.

One of the problems of cubism, and especially analytical cubism, as Clement Greenberg pointed out, was that in their paintings cubists had difficulty with the corners. He said, 'They make round pictures.' But now it's dawned on me why they had difficulty with the corners. I've discovered why through doing this photography. In the picture that has four edges, the edges are the most interesting, the sides particularly, because the top is the sky – infinity, or a roof – and the bottom is you, your feet, your body. But we don't *see* that way at all. I realized that with this photography I was making

things closer to the truth of the way we see things. We see everything in focus, everything, but we don't see it all at once, that's the point. We take time. The camera, the one-eyed camera, can be arranged so that it sees a lot in focus, but it's difficult if there's something very close to it and there's something else thirty feet away.

It is possible to do this technically. If I look at your face I can also see this tape recorder. It's not blurred, nothing is blurred. If I move my eyes and look at the tape recorder I can see a great deal more, but now your face is different. It isn't blurred, though, nothing is ever blurred, unless there is something wrong with your eyes, and then you would wear spectacles. Blurred things are unnatural, we don't see that way, nobody does. In the photograph you often get blur, and therefore in time they'll come to be seen as slightly primitive images, I'm sure. Again, you're dealing with this urge for verisimilitude – a natural urge because it does seem that there's a truth there. I realized that although it looks as if the cubists were abstracting, what they were really trying to do was to ask: 'what is it I see when I look at your face, and how do I deal with it?'

At one time I said I was going to take pictures with peripheral vision, but you can't do that, you'd drive yourself insane! But in painting, of course, you can, and this may be the area where vision merges with other senses – memory, for instance – and gets very complicated. These ideas encouraged me to look again at cubist pictures, which I began to see in a different light. I was more and more fascinated. Cubism, which is a great idea about reality, has not influenced realist painting much outside Picasso and Braque, and the people who were involved. I think that is because Picasso is such a giant artist. It's difficult to deal with these giant human beings, we tend to skirt around them. You can see in painting today it's as though Picasso hadn't been there. But this giant was there and we must deal with him. The influence of Picasso was superficial in the sense that people hadn't grasped fully what he was doing. They did know it was interesting, but they could only deal with the superficial aspects of what had happened. Therefore Picassoesque painting emerged. It was then I realized that I was attempting two-eyed photo-

graphy, and that while I was taking the photographs I was spending a great deal of time looking, but not through the camera.

Ordinarily the photographer spends the time looking through the camera because he needs that frame. I began to realize that I was making pictures in a very strange way, in that when I began I did not know where the edge was going to be. Now, in any drawing or painting you know where the edge is because you begin on a piece of paper, or canvas, anything, but it's got four edges. No matter what you do on it the four sides make it into something, and so a few marks can, for instance, suggest a landscape. Oddly enough this is not like a window, even though it looks literal enough, because your eye is moving in and out all the time as it does naturally. I may be perfectly still but my eye is moving around the room and wherever it moves everything is in focus. I am literally taking the photograph and the viewer's eye perceives this, which is the reason for things appearing to move in and out. You could use a telephoto to do this, but there isn't one on this Pentax 110 – I've only got one extra little lens. You literally walk about, and then the eye of the spectator does the same thing, giving this incredible spatial effect. These joiners are more spatial in feeling than any stereoscopic photograph, aren't they?

PJ: Well, those are dead and fixed. And they have to be hard-edged to get that three-dimensional effect.

DH: I realized suddenly, you're moving! And that, unlike an ordinary photograph, the composition of the finished picture with the joiners was not as important in terms of *making you look*. In an ordinary photograph, a one-eyed photograph, composition in many ways is everything, and the only thing that can transcend this is a face. If you have a face depicted, the features and the things that it tells you are more interesting than what is happening at the side. Something strongly erotic would have this effect too. Otherwise, it's the edges that are making you look, and lines from there often lead you into the picture – that's what the photographer uses. The painter uses these devices as well to make you look here or there. Suddenly I realized that I could have gone on and

made another side here, another on the top, another on the bottom, and it wouldn't have affected greatly the quality achieved already. Each individual photograph, of course, is thoughtfully composed. And again, this was a new discovery, and related to the problems unearthed by cubism. Cubism was total vision: it was about two eyes and the way we see things. Photography had the flaw of being one-eyed, which I had sensed, but not pinpointed, really. The moment you break that down there are amazing possibilities.

I'm convinced now that there is no such thing as objective vision. We choose all the time what we see, and different things make us look. We realize that we are always attracted to certain things. In any picture, if there is a figure big enough we are forced to look at it, but if there is a face, then you cannot *not* look at it. And if there are strong eyes in a painting or photograph you are drawn to them.

The other thing we are drawn and attracted to is light, until it reaches the point where it is too strong, and then we are repelled and have to turn away. Apart from these things, there are other reasons for looking. *What* do you see? *How* do you see? I notice that people who come in here to see me are mostly people who are interested in visual art, they are curious people who look around a lot. I tend to do that, I notice things. Each person notices different things first, but everybody sees people first. You look at people, or you deliberately don't look. If you don't look, it's a very conscious choice you make. And then, of course, if you were a painter, you'd look at the paint, and if you were a book dealer you'd look at the books, and so on and so on. Different people would choose different things depending on their interests and ideas. All vision must be like this in some way, something attracting us while other things repel. The moment that you leave cubism and this whole area, you have the problem about the one eye, and then everything becomes based on a fixed point. My joke was that all ordinary photographs are taken by a one-eyed frozen man! But the joiners are to do with movement. I'm moving around when I'm taking them. For instance, it's not possible to use a tripod, not the way I'm working.

PJ: Well, you'd be there for three days, wouldn't you?

Christopher Isherwood and Don Bachardy (painting 1968)

DH: Oh, yes! Unbelievable! You'd go mad. You just couldn't do it.

PJ: You say that you have reached the end of your three months of intense work on this, but do you see yourself pursuing it?

DH: Well, yes, but I want to put these ideas back into painting – it might take me months of hard work, but I could discover another kind of cubism. Cubism isn't a style: it's an attitude. Treating it as a style, people simply imitated what Picasso had experienced, and if you use your own experience eventually you come up with something different. His example is too good, too complicated to avoid, but if you look at it more than superficially, you realize what was going on. This work has made me do that. I knew the joiners were related to drawing because you have to know where to put things. You have to know about drawing.

PJ: I see what you mean about the graphic problems. Is the centre your starting point? Do you move from there outwards? The structuring of these photographic pieces must present you with complex problems.

Don and Christopher, Los Angeles,
6th March 1982 (Polaroid collage)

DH: I move from faces outwards. In the portrait of Don [Bachardy] and Christopher [Isherwood], for instance, I started with the faces, but I move and change about. Don was looking at me, but I noticed that he kept looking at Christopher. This is about the second double portrait as a joiner that I did. And even though things have got out of scale, you're aware that he's watching Christopher, aren't you?

PJ: Yes, you are. And in your famous portrait of him it's the reverse! These photographs really show that we look at people in a series of glances: look at them, then away, look back, and so on.

DH: Yes, and I think that's why these have a dimension that hasn't been seen before. This is scrutiny, and it took time.

In December 1983 Hockney delivered his first lecture on photography in England at the Victoria and Albert Museum. The lecture was, on the whole, well received, but other photographers (such as David Bailey, who left the auditorium with embarrassing speed) failed to engage Hockney in the kind of provocative questioning he had hoped for. However, the audience was respectful and attentive, and there was not a seat to be had in the room.

His photographic show at the Hayward Gallery in London (9 November 1983–5 February 1984) drew record crowds, although the general level of critical commentary was depressingly low. We met briefly during the few days he was in London, and agreed to continue our conversations. David's pleasure at the public reaction to the show was somewhat blunted by the negative response to his work from the photographic establishment.

During the winter of 1983 we spoke frequently on the telephone, and it was clear that his passionate engagement with photography continued unabated. He constantly expressed surprise that his ideas for the joiners were not being taken up. Again and again I would gently point out that photographers would hardly embrace a technique which seemed to undermine their own practices, and which required a true artistic sensibility and an ability to draw. David kept hoping for a more positive response.

George Lawson and Wayne Sleep,
Pembroke Studios, London, 1st May 1982
(Polaroid collage)

Los Angeles:
May 1984

In May 1984 I flew to Los Angeles to research a film on the actor and director Dennis Hopper, who made his reputation with Easy Rider *in 1968. The very day I arrived Hopper was taken into hospital. I was able to visit David at his home off Mulholland Drive almost daily for the next three weeks, which made for a special intensity in our dialogue. Although he had recently constructed an enormous studio in his garden by razing a tennis court, the whole house is effectively his workspace. Space is one of the reasons Hockney has now committed himself fully to Los Angeles. Much of his work in progress would be brought down to the living room, which has a magnificent terrace running the length of the house, overlooking the famous pool. Here it would be studied, tried out in frames, and pinned to the wall. We would sit surrounded by David's work and discuss photography and the problems of seeing.*

PJ: Can we talk about the differences between Western and Eastern notions of perspective? If a conventional Western perspective freezes the moment, it must surely stop the flow of time.

DH: It must do. In that Chinese book,* which I found so fascinating, it says that perspective must be read laterally. On a flat surface, it is just about all the eye can do, but the surface tells you things: it gives you illusions. Perspective makes you think of deep space on a flat surface. But the trouble with perspective is that it has no movement at all. The one vanishing point exists only for a fraction of a second to us. The moment your eye moves slightly, it's gone, and it's somewhere else. In a painting, the hand is moving, the mark is being made: these things themselves run through time.

Why is it that people are always interested and impressed by what they call 'hand-done' work? The camera is only a machine, but a drawing made by a human machine fascinates them much more than anything photographic. It's an interesting fact that the perspective in painting matters less than it does in the photograph which is forced to have perspective. I did make one photograph without perspective† but you have to literally move in order to do that. The joiners have many perspectives within one general one. You sit still, so you have the feeling of a general perspective, but the moment your head moves there are many more.

PJ: Such as in your picture of the Ryoanji Gardens?‡

DH: Yes . . . I'm positive now that what we see depends also on our memory. The Renaissance idea of fixing space persists – posing for a photograph is a Renaissance idea! When you pose for the picture you stop, and you imitate this stopped time. But it's the only time we do that, for an artist or a photograph. Otherwise we move. When I took the picture at Ryoanji, I planned it. After all, the garden as we know it is a rectangle. Because it's on a different plane, at ninety degrees to us, we can know it to be a rectangle only by moving along it. If you visit the garden, and you are not photographing it, you would walk along the edge of it, sit down, contemplate, do whatever you are supposed to do. And when you had left, if someone asked you what shape it was, you would say it was a rectangle. Now, if you had seen it from one point, as in the other photograph I took, you would think it was a triangle.

---

* *Principles of Chinese Painting* by George Rowley (Princeton University Press, 1959).

† 'Walking in the Zen Garden at the Ryoanji Temple, Kyoto, February 21st 1983' (see page 58).
‡ The Ryoanji Garden in Kyoto, Japan, one of the oldest and most renowned of all the Zen gardens, was probably laid out by the tea master and painter Soami, who was active in the late fifteenth century.

So we come back to a weird question: when is the present? When did the past end and the present occur, and when does the future start? This is a very strange area, and it must affect everything. It certainly affects shape. It leads you to something weird and disturbing, because we haven't *seen* that way yet. The only people who can make us see are not scientists, but artists. This is why Picasso is so interesting. He always questioned how we see. A great deal of other art simply accepts a way of seeing. Certainly, ordinary photography has one way of seeing only, which is fixed, as if there is a kind of objective reality, which simply cannot be. I'm becoming aware that we can move into another consciousness. That's where I think Picasso was moving. That's why he was so excited, why he couldn't stop work. He knew that every time you look there's something different. There is so much *there*, but we're not seeing it, that's the problem. And we're moving into what would be a new experience for us which goes beyond art, I do think that.

Unfortunately, science, for the purpose of illustrating things, is still geared to the inventions of art, and has been since science and art were together in the Renaissance. Consequently, we have machines to depict things, the camera itself of course. The only way scientists can make depictions is by using a computer, but it is still essentially from a fixed point of view. The computer itself can't see: it can only be programmed.

PJ: I wonder whether you are going almost beyond art itself, or art as we know it, into an area of representation which we haven't even thought about?

DH: Don't you think it's possible? It must be possible, because we become more and more aware; we do make advances. But at times I feel I must be going mad, it's all so strange. On the other hand, something new would be very strange to us at the beginning. A great deal of the art of the past wasn't made as art. We are self-conscious about it now. We say it's art, but artists didn't always claim that: they were simply telling us about things they saw. There is art which people say is primitive, but it's actually highly sophisticated and much closer to reality than the photograph can be.

Sitting in the Rock Garden at the Ryoanji Temple, Kyoto, February 1983 (photographic collage)

PJ: Yes, really ancient art often shows people living and working, the daily problems of existing in a hostile world. It deals with mythology, too, and photography rarely does that.

DH: The experience of art is more real, the moment is longer, and we can feel that moment, but in a photograph we can't. Perhaps this is why there are so few good photographs, and those good ones that do exist are almost accidental, one fraction of a second that looks as though it's longer than it is. We don't know what a fraction of a second is, stopped,

isolated. We can't isolate a second in our lives, can we? So the photograph must be a much more primitive picture than a painting is. But, if you asked the average person which looks more real, they would say the photograph. I'm convinced it can't be true.

PJ: So-called reality accords with a programmed way of looking which goes back to what you were saying earlier, that the photograph has influenced the way we look. If we are presented with a photograph, we say: well, that's life. But it may not only be still photographs that are responsible for that. Movies have influenced our way of seeing as well, but they are not life at all. They show a world confected, glamorized, changed.

DH: I do think it's true that all depictions must be stylized, what we would call stylized. There is no way they can't be. After all, they are not the reality. They are put on a flat surface as stylizations of some kind.

Listen to this [quotes from Leo Steinberg*]:

Surveying Picasso's lifelong commitment to the theme of woman as solid reality – a commitment relaxed only during the cubist episode – one arrives at a disturbing conclusion. That Picasso, the great flattener of twentieth-century painting, has had to cope in himself with the most uncompromising three-dimensional imagination that ever possessed a great painter. And that he flattened the language of painting in the years just before World War I because the traditional means of 3D rendering inherited from the past were for him too one-sided, too lamely content with the exclusive aspect. In other words – not 3D enough.

Amazing, isn't it! Picasso shows you both front and back, and this must be about memory because . . .

PJ: You must retain one when you are looking at the other. Of course, when we walk round an object, such as a jacket

---

that's on a peg, we are also dealing with what we *expect* it to be like. We have seen a jacket before and our imagination and our memory are stimulated by something already seen and known.

DH: Yes, once you've seen something before it remains in your memory. And as time passed, a few seconds ago, *that's* your memory, it's all accumulating in us, isn't it?

The rendering of that figure has become so apt and effortless that it belies the burden of the attempt. It accords with Picasso's oft-quoted remark – 'I don't seek, I find.' But such euphoric statements must be read against the more frequent kind: 'One never stops seeking because one never finds anything.' Or: 'I never do a painting as a work of art. All of them are researches. I search constantly, and there is a logical sequence in all this research. It's an experiment in time.'

I'd never read that before, but it must be, of course, because if you're putting a front and back together to make it one, they work as one. And remember, only thirty years ago many people, intelligent people, attacked Picasso's drawing, saying it was distorted and horrible. It isn't distorted, actually. There's no distortion. He taught us to see a great deal more, at least he did me. But thirty years ago they all said: people just don't look like that. They said that because they could only take one moment, the way something looks in a fixed perspective. But after throwing it up in 1904 or so he then spent nearly seventy years, working every day, pursuing the problems of depiction in a way that nobody else has. And if it took *him* seventy years . . . Picasso's work is there: we have to learn from it. Art that doesn't take in his work I think is just a waste, although it may be pleasurable. I know his work is important, even though it may be hard to grasp.

PJ: How do you grasp time? You can't. But for me there's only one other artist who comes close to Picasso and that's Rembrandt. He builds time into his self-portraits so that the man appears to age visibly as we look at the paintings.

---

* *Other Criteria* by Leo Steinberg (Oxford University Press, 1975).

DH: Oddly enough, you're picking two artists there who both have incredible humanity.

PJ: And they are not frightened of examining their own faults, either. What excited me about Picasso's later lithographic work was seeing him come to terms with his age and his sexuality and his time in the world.

DH: Of course, of course, and as you go on the memories are accumulating in your head all the time. They tell us that brain cells are dying, but things do go in and stay there, piling up. As Picasso got older and older he got somehow more and more energetic, and more and more things happened in his work. When you begin to understand what he was doing a bit, you are hardly surprised he couldn't stop, the work was much too interesting. There is nothing else like it: no other artist got anywhere near it. Strangely enough, people didn't see it! I never doubted Picasso, I never doubted his integrity, and I never believed for one moment that he just churned out stuff which was all the same. If people say those things, they are proving that they don't understand his work.

I don't think money meant anything to Picasso, or fame or vanity, for that matter. Even the vanity of an artist which, after all, is a strong feeling. Picasso was on his own. Nobody else has really got away from that vision we think we see. And that vision has got more pervasive in the years since cubism. Photographs now surround us, daily they go through everybody's letter box inside newspapers. In 1904 there were fewer photographs around, but now they are everywhere.

It's interesting that now the Chinese would not make a scroll if they wanted to depict, for instance, their leader making a visit to the South, and the picture wouldn't be as good. It wouldn't tell you as much. People don't believe me, but I have seen the evidence. It's a bit mind-blowing, and it goes way outside technology, which is very refreshing!

PJ: You were saying earlier that you thought photography was not the beginning of something, but rather the end …

DH: That is clear to me now. And I explained this to Colin Ford.* He said it was all very interesting but, after all, he had this photographic museum and all these old photographs!

Well, I said, I'm not suggesting you throw them away! They are interesting, they are documents, and if you have a museum, then put them in. But it is the end of something and not the beginning. I'm not suggesting photography is nothing. But it is the end because it is the end of a way of seeing that was developed five hundred years ago.

The more you think it out the more obvious it becomes. Perspective is a theoretical abstraction that was worked out in the fifteenth century. It suddenly altered pictures: it gave a strong illusion of depth; it lost something and gained something. At first the gain was thrilling, but slowly, very slowly, we became aware of what had been lost. That loss was the depiction of the passing of time. We thought this way of looking was so true that when the photograph came along it seemed to confirm perspective. Of course, it was going to confirm perspective because it was exactly the same way of looking, from one central point with one eye fixed in time.

We know perspective is not real: we know the lines don't meet; we know that if you move along them all is parallel. Clearly the photograph belongs to the Renaissance picture. Cubism is the only thing that's broken the grip of the old perspective. When you look at old cubism, you realize how primitive that is, but, obviously, it can move on. The fact that all those years passed and we didn't quite grasp what was going on is neither here nor there. In many ways it doesn't matter.

I tried to break the old perspective with the joiners and, even then, sometimes they succeed and sometimes they don't. The important thing was that those experiments with photography led me back to the hand. In fragmenting perspective I had then to piece it together. You need the hand to piece it together because, essentially, you are drawing. It's not then the little mechanical instrument you are using: if you're drawing there are many choices, many ways to put the joiners together. Other people put them together very simply because they can't draw, it comes down to that.

Picasso, however, moved on. He didn't go back to the

---

* Colin Ford, Keeper, National Museum of Photography, Film and Television, Bradford.

previous ways of showing time passing, such as the Chinese scroll. And apart from Picasso, the Chinese scrolls are the most sophisticated images I've ever seen. Stunning! How vivid the experience was! It was one of the most thrilling days I've ever had.*

We were on the floor, going along the scroll, and the man there began to tell me about certain special courtiers who wore little red hats. And I said: yes we passed the shop that was selling them a few feet back along the scroll there! Now, you couldn't say that about a Canaletto. You don't make a tour of an ordinary painting in that way. You don't go into it. You're still a spectator outside it, essentially. With the scrolls, you are *in* there, as though you had passed the shop back there on the street, a little shop with hats piled up, unbeliev-

ably vivid! And it's interesting that you'd use language like that, you'd say: yes, I passed the shop; because you literally had passed it and gone on to something else. How many pictures can you talk about like that? Even in a movie, the photographer has to actually show you things, but here, you *choose* to stop somewhere, and that act shows you that it's a vastly different way of making a picture.

I don't think Picasso ever saw those scrolls. Very few people have seen them. You can't just go in: you have to ask to see them in the British Museum in London, or in the Metropolitan Museum in New York. The National Gallery

---

* Hockney viewed a Chinese scroll at the Sydney Moss Gallery, Brook Street, London.

From Wu-hsi to Suchou, the seventh Nan-hsün-t'u handscroll, by Wang Hui, 1691–8

has now bought a cubist painting. It's quite different from all the other pictures in the gallery, for most of them are concerned with the old ways of seeing, and this fact will have to be explained in the National Gallery itself. It is a scholars' problem; on the surface it looks as if there's a connection, but the way of seeing has changed. A photograph would fit into that gallery just as the Renaissance pictures do.

PJ: In fact, the National Portrait Gallery, just around the corner, has a huge collection of photographs, and they fit very well with the paintings.

DH: And they do fit well because most photographic portraits have been posed in exactly the same way.

PJ: And, unfortunately, most photographic portraits are superior to most painted portraits now, simply because there are so few good artists.

DH: And most of the pap painters use photographs, you can tell. They've got all the faults of the photographic portrait and all the faults of the lousy hand and brush, which makes it worse! There's the guy who does Prince Charles . . .

PJ: Orchid, or someone, Organ . . .

DH: That's it, Bryan Organ. Terrible, absolutely terrible.

PJ: I don't understand why those people are commissioned to paint portraits.

DH: Because nobody thinks about it. Tradition tells them that the painted portrait should be better. Some painted portraits *are* superb. If Rembrandt were here, you wouldn't compare. But Organ is nowhere near Rembrandt; the photographs would be better. But nobody would admit that: they would have to start thinking first. You can't expect somebody at Buckingham Palace to start thinking this out. Their way of thinking is completely fixed. I try to talk to people but they never come back. I say things, hoping that they are outrageous. I did a little essay for a show called 'The Artist's Eye'*

---

* 'The Artist's Eye' exhibition, National Gallery, 1 July–31 August 1981.

last year, and in it I made the provocative suggestion that photography was only good for reproducing drawings and paintings, but nobody took it up.

PJ: That whole lecture of yours is provocative. People choose to ignore that. I'm a very traditional photographer, but I recognize that this is something too important to ignore. It has to be pursued. The issues go far beyond photography.

DH: I know that.

PJ: Photography is just the excuse, but in a sense, it is photography which is holding us back from talking further.

DH: Absolutely. When I'm attacking photography I'm attacking the traditional view. I'm sure people don't really think the photograph is objective reality, do they?

PJ: Well, it depends. Those in the Fine Art end of photography would not hold that view, but a lot of people would say: that is a real object that was perceived to be like that at the time, so it must be an objective record.

If you take, for example, photographers such as W. H. Jackson, Eadweard Muybridge or Timothy O'Sullivan, the pioneers of American photography, many of them went out to shoot landscape photographs when the railroads were being constructed. And those photographs were sent back as examples of objective reality. In fact, they were some of the best landscape photographs ever taken because they were taken very simply. Beautiful large-format pictures. Those photographers are now being promoted as artists, indeed some of them saw quite magnificently, but they were simply commissioned to record what they saw.

DH: You must remember that a great deal of the art of the past was not made as art.

PJ: Well, those photographs certainly weren't, they were pure documentary records.

DH: But we know that people who took them were artists. We can tell: the photographs still work for us although they weren't made self-consciously as art. That self-consciousness is late nineteenth or early twentieth century.

Mammoth Hot Springs on Gardiner's River
by W. H. Jackson *c.* 1880

Cathedral Rock, 2600 ft, Yosemite,
by C. E. Watkins, 1866

PJ: Why do you think Picasso, who was surrounded by people who took photographs, and certainly knew Man Ray, never took up photography himself?

DH: Well, Alain Sayag told me, when I had started the Polaroids, that Picasso had said the only thing to do with the camera was to just move it around.

PJ: Like you do.

DH: I think that's true. As I said, the idea of the camera on the tripod is a Renaissance idea, the drawing machine with the one hole and the man looking through it. It does create a distance effect. The great difference between the Chinese scholar-artist and Renaissance scholar-artist is this: if the Chinese scholar-artist had a garden, however small that garden was, he would want to walk in it, so he would make his path so that he'd have a longer walk. So he walks up the path of his garden and then goes and makes a picture of that garden, or the experience of walking in it. But the Renais-sance scholar sits in a room and looks out of a window, and then makes his picture.

He is fixed there with the window-picture, and therefore he thinks of perspective. The Chinese wouldn't because their experience is moving, flowing, as time is flowing. And so they both start off with very different locations; one is seated and the other is not. He might sit down to make his picture, but his picture is not *of* being seated but of walking in the garden. Then you suddenly see the difference, and see where one leads, and the other leads. If only the Chinese had invented a camera, that would have been something!

PJ: We talked about the camera obscura, which was an early device, hundreds of years before an emulsion was able to represent what it saw, but what about before that – was the artist still looking out of a window?

DH: Before the fifteenth century, no: before the so-called primitives, you have lateral movement; the story *is* told

The Ambassadors by Hans Holbein

moving about. You move along, and that way things appear less solid.

PJ: Two-dimensional?

DH: Yes. In doing that you have the advantage of time. But in wanting to make it solid you must stop time, that's the problem, the core of the problem, isn't it? In creating depth you ...

PJ: ... abolish time.

DH: Yes, but it looks solid, so we think, it's more like it is. Well, there's a point to it that's half true, but the sacrifice you have to make is the experience of the flow of time, which, in the end is more important to us. That's life!

PJ: But what about a picture like Holbein's 'The Ambassadors', which must be the apotheosis of that viewpoint?

DH: Holbein must have used the camera obscura because that skull is the distortion you achieve with a camera. You can't make that up. It's so perfect when you look down at it.

PJ: Yes, I've seen it through a movie camera which can bring it into focus.

DH: It's simple. Holbein was playing, enjoying games with what appeared to be this new, wonderful instrument which was helping the depiction of reality. It's true, the figures suddenly seem more solid, even today – we would say (and I nearly say it myself) more real. But we must not say that because it simply isn't true.

PJ: Maybe that's one of the few exceptions. And it is an exceptional picture.

DH: Oh, it's a beautiful picture! The other weird conclusion I came to, and this may seem really contradictory, was that abstraction didn't come from cubism, but from the Renaissance picture. Cubism actually opens up narrative again: it is about time, but we have been told that it's the other way around. If you think about it, the fixing of shapes because of perspective did limit narrative in painting more and more from the fifteenth century on. And so telling a story got more

Bacchus and Ariadne by Titian

and more difficult. You had to pick one part of the story: you had to stop it. All right, you got solid people in it, but take Titian's 'Bacchus and Ariadne' in the National Gallery, where the figures are frozen, the great cloak flowing in the sky. It can only contain one or, at the most, two events.

With perspective people began to pose, as they do, even today, for the photograph. 'Sitting' it's called! And, slowly, it made narrative more and more difficult pictorially until, finally, you got one kind of illustrative action; that's all you could deal with. Whereas cubism opened up such incredible narrative possibilities that I think I can understand the frenzy of Picasso's work. Of course, you wouldn't stop. You'd just keep on. I think his work will go on revealing itself. Leo Steinberg says this:

The staggering corpus of Picasso's production seems still to be opening up, the familiar reappears undiscovered. I am convinced that all of Picasso's work needs re-thinking in the light of the whole; that the prevailing trend to dismiss work done after the thirties is misconceived; and that the significant unity of Picasso's creation will become ever clearer, so that even his cubism will eventually come to seem more like the rest of Picasso and less like the cubism of other men. Above all, I believe that, like the rhetoric of adulation, the professional criticism of our century has been busily shielding us from the onslaught of Picasso's imagination.

People want to make things neat all the time but life isn't like that.

PJ: And they always want to say about an artist: well, his earlier work was better than his later, or his middle period was more exciting, just to put a value on things, so that they can say that the later pictures aren't worth owning.

DH: It's more about commerce, than art, really, but it should be about something really important that would enrich us all, make experience more vivid. I think so. I keep groping.

PJ: What is it that photography has failed to do, do you think? Has it a fundamental flaw?

DH: Photography *has* failed. I talked in the Picasso lecture* about the documentary nature of photography precisely because we think it's a good documentary medium. Well, there it has failed. I had seen it already in the Chinese scroll of the journey. I said a movie couldn't be as good, and any photographic documentation couldn't be as good as that scroll. You don't experience photographs in that way.

Photography has almost failed to capture our time in the world. After all, the way that a really good photograph works is that it sticks in your head. Different photographs stick in different people's heads. A photograph of my mother and father, a rather ordinary little snapshot, might stick in my head whereas it might not stick in yours. It's not necessarily the quality, the way the image was made, it's something else. I am simply adding more to them in my mind, and for each

person different pictures must trigger different responses.

How many truly *memorable* pictures are there? Considering the millions of photographs taken, there are few memorable images in this medium, which should tell us something. There have been far more images made this way than the sum of all previous images put together.

Twentieth-century art is so self-conscious that it has isolated itself as if it were a completely separate activity. I've heard very serious people say some strange things to me. I had an argument once with Suzi Gablik† who said to me, well, art isn't for everybody. And I said that if I believed that, I think I'd shoot myself! It can't be true. I said to her: you've reduced it to the level of jewellery, frankly. Jewellery isn't for everybody, and it doesn't matter, it's not that important. But art is not on that level, it's on a much higher one. She was maybe suggesting that people are too dumb, but this cannot be true either. How do you then account for the fact that all societies, even primitive societies, make art? We all need it. It may be that the vast majority of people appreciate only very low art, but it is still art.

Without images how would I know what you see? I don't know what you see. I'll never know, but these flat images are the only things that connect up between us. Just because we don't bump into each other, it doesn't mean that we all see the same thing, does it? Obviously some people see more — maybe their profession makes them see more, it could be just that. Photographers, painters may see more because they are looking for more. I think that Picasso saw more than anybody else. The evidence is strong.

I'm suggesting photography should be attacked partly because it has an official position. If it didn't have that official position it might be slightly different, but it does have all over the world. Photographs have become necessary to identify things. This presents a way of seeing that it suggests is the official and right way. Well that's what I'm criticizing, essentially. Photography doesn't get nearer experience. Painting gets nearer to it because it can do far more. Its way of seeing can extend all the time because it's related to *us*. And that's

---

* Given at the Los Angeles County Museum of Art in 1982.

† Suzi Gablik, writer and critic.

where the hand comes in – then we know our own body is dealing with it. I don't think people have really attacked photography before, they don't bother! And possibly there was no reason to before. I had no reason to, but the more thought you give it the more reason there is for attacking it. When I say attacking, I'm really suggesting a debate. Let's start discussing it. The world of painting almost stopped the debate. It went off on its own. There's Man Ray's comment, 'I photograph what you can't paint, and I paint what you can't photograph.' That's very good. It's a start!

Now, apart from the other problem with the photograph, there is a pictorial flaw – the lack of the hand, it all boils down to that. When I suggested that you couldn't look at a photograph for very long the way you could a painting, that photography does not have the ambiguities that art has – all that came about because of my realization of what I call the flaw. And the flaw gets more and more obvious the bigger you make the picture. In the Anthropology Museum in Mexico City* there are some very, very large photographs, and the bigger they are the flatter they seem. Partly this is to do with scale, because your eye has to move from one corner to

---

* Hockney made various visits to Mexico between 1984 and 1986.

another. You are moving through time and the image is not. But any *drawn* image is moving through time because of the hand at work. So I think that flaw is serious, although it can be overcome by the techniques I use myself, and then the experience of looking at something is much more parallel to real experience. Now in the work I did they are certainly not all the same. I think there's a clear progression of complexity arising, the more you realize what you can do with it. The last ones are the most complex and the most satisfying, I think. These are getting closer to experience – I'm moving about more and more, which means you have to remember not only where you've been and what you've photographed, but where you were when you took the photograph. You have to train your memory to do these joiners. The great big Grand Canyon photographs trained my eye to see things in a certain way. Photographing the world's biggest hole, you are photographing space. We can't comprehend space itself, it's infinite, but we can glimpse it in the huge hole of the Grand Canyon.

Obviously, there are limitations with this work: the photograph can't make the picture as I'm making that painting there. I have to go somewhere with a camera to photograph something. With painting I don't, and that means there's something more going on in the head. That's the exciting

The Grand Canyon Looking North 11, September 1982, Collage No 2, made May 1986 (photographic collage)

The Grand Canyon Looking North, September 1982
(photographic collage)

thing to me, and the reason I stopped using the camera and went back to painting.

Of course, photography completely altered my painting. Although I said I was drawing when I made the joiners, the work I was doing was also photography. It was made with a camera and with what I know of photography. In another sense it is drawing because you are making choices all the time, and the choices seemed to me to be the kinds of choices you make when you are drawing. It might appear that you're cutting down what's there, but actually you are finding out more of what is there. It's like editing, really.

In this roundabout way I'm saying that the photograph can't lead us to a new way of seeing. It may have other possibilities but only painting can extend the way of seeing. I think it's becoming apparent to some people now.

PJ: It is apparent to me, and that's why I'm pursuing this so rigorously. I know there's a fundamental flaw with photography, but I have never been able to understand it properly. I am understanding it much better now that you've explained your thoughts and backed up your position with such revolutionary work.

DH: I couldn't have made those statements without the work. I've heard people say: I don't think much of photography! Alan Bowness of the Tate Gallery has said that to me. On the other hand, he couldn't state why. It would be difficult to make my case without something positive. I suggested my work was a critique of photography made with photography. After all, it's no good using language to do it. You've got to use the photographic language.

Certainly, the pictures are difficult: true art can be difficult. Cubism must have seemed very difficult and strange to a great number of people – it looked as if things were being smashed up, whereas, actually, it was the opposite. Things looked strange because it was a different way of seeing, a different way of making a depiction. People had been used to another way that had seemed to be real. It looks a lot less strange to us now, even though many people think it's not reality. But cubism has a long way to go. My photographs should make people look at cubism a little differently.

PJ: They have. They are both commentaries on and extrapolations from cubism.

DH: People should go back to cubism more. Somebody told me it was a pity they didn't have my show before the big cubist exhibition at the Tate Gallery* because more people would have gone to it. I thought it was the best cubist show ever put on. I went eight times: I thought it was absolutely thrilling. I got such a feeling of closeness.

I'm sure that not many photographers would have thought of going to the cubist show. They would not have thought it relevant in any way. But I'm sure good photographers look at painting. Cartier-Bresson must have done: he trained as a draughtsman. I would have thought that anybody who is interested in pictures would be interested in photographs. I said there had been no cubist photography, and the photographic historians attacked me for that. But I'd still say it because I think what they call cubist photography is very superficial.

PJ: They were simply using abstract shapes.

DH: Yes, shapes and shadows and so on. I wouldn't call that cubist photography. I don't think many painters, or even many critics of painting, would call it cubist work. Douglas Cooper, who organized the cubist show, would dismiss it. After all, he was dismissing a lot of other painting that would claim to be cubist. I can see what he meant. It takes a long time to understand cubism fully. The advantage in photography is that people do *believe* the photograph: they believe it was made in a certain way, and they believe the photographer was there, essentially. Here's a story about this.

Last Christmas I was in London, and Mark Haworth-Booth† had come round to get me to talk on the tape recorder about Bill Brandt's photographs, specifically those in the book *Literary Britain*. Many of the photographs are very

---

* 'The Essential Cubism, 1907–20', Tate Gallery 27 April–31 July 1983.
† Mark Haworth-Booth, Assistant Keeper, Department of Prints, Drawing and Photography, Victoria and Albert Museum.

striking – there's one of Top Withens in Yorkshire, which is a very dramatic photograph. I was looking at this one for quite a while, and I started asking him some questions about it. I said: there's one thing I've noticed that's strange – there's a very bright light in the sky back there, but the grass in the foreground has also got a very bright light coming towards it here. He must have used a flash of some sort, otherwise, where was the light coming from? And he said: ah, the sky is from another negative.

Well, this horrified me, and I suggested this was Stalinist photography. It was a collage, really, but there was no evidence of it being a collage. There's nothing wrong with collage at all, but it should be quite clear that one thing is stuck on top of another. This photograph was not like that, and so people would assume that it had been made from a single image. When you can tell that the sky is from another day and yet you pretend that it's not, then I think you can talk about Stalinist photography. The reason that Stalinism works in photography is that we do believe what is there in front of us. When Trotsky's next to Lenin, and then he's taken out, they are suggesting that Trotsky was not there at all. Painting is not the same. You can paint a picture of Lenin making a speech and never put Trotsky there, just as though you never noticed him. But the camera is not like this, and so you're back to the point that what you depict should be in front of you. So these techniques seem deceitful to me.

Then Mark said: what does it matter as long as you get a good picture? Well, I said: wouldn't it have been more honest to have just clipped the thing on? And then I thought about it, and realized that with my technique it would be very difficult to make Stalinist photography. What I'm saying is not just out of the back of my head: I've thought about all this and made experiments and done things to prove what I suggest. I've no doubt that there will be great opposition to what I say, just as there was a kind of academy that opposed a great deal of change in the way of *seeing* in painting. I think the opposition will be stronger in photography. But I think the advertisers will be the first to take up these techniques. They will realize that people's eyes can be held longer with the joiners.

PJ: I've already seen a very bad rip-off of your ideas. A brandy manufacturer showing the inside of a room, all yellow, with the perspective all over the place.

DH: I've no doubt, I think that's the way it would happen first, but even if it's a bad rip-off, if it works enough for people to notice it then something is happening.

PJ: It's easy to look at the surface of what you do and try to

Lenin Addressing a Meeting in Moscow The figure to the right of the podium is Trotsky who was subsequently eliminated from official versions of this photograph

reproduce that, but I don't think those photographs are to do with surface at all.

DH: I talk a great deal about surface in 'The Artist's Eye' booklet. But then I suggested that what's behind the surface you can begin to get in the reproduction as well. It's a simple truth, I think, but it needed saying, and that's why a reproduction can give joy; the art still works.

PJ: What you say is going to be much more important to painters, or should I say to real artists, and that excludes most photographers. I think you're using photography to address a much wider audience.

DH: I am, I'm suggesting that painting should again do certain things, it should be telling us about the visible world. Picasso was always telling us about the visible world, he never went away from it. That's no accident, you know, there's a good, solid, sound reason for it. And I'm speaking to myself, for my own painting, but I'm also speaking to others.

The great pity now is that you need something like the Royal Academy was, but is no longer. When it was founded, frankly, most of the good artists of the day were either members of it or they exhibited there. It was an organization of artists run completely by artists. There were no critics, there were no curators, there were no people who were not involved in both the theory and the practice of painting. The Royal Academy today is not like that. It's become a charming, idiosyncratic little place, but nobody takes it very seriously.

Only artists look at late Picasso and see what's there, because only artists can do something about it. They are the only ones with influence. A curator can't influence anybody. All he can do is write books. It must come from artists. If our generation doesn't deal with this another will. It's too rich, it's too interesting. If the Royal Academy was real, it too would know that. I'm not criticizing; I'm simply saying it's anachronistic.

When they put on, for instance, 'A New Spirit in Painting' show at the Royal Academy, I went in one night just before it opened and Howard Hodgkin was hanging his pictures. The people who organized the exhibition suggested he take one of the pictures out: they didn't like it. And I said to Howard, who quite liked it: I wouldn't take it out. You just keep it there. If they ask you again, just say you'll take the lot out and leave an empty room. They'll notice Howard Hodgkin's empty room! Anyway, Howard took it out in the end. And I argued with David Sylvester,* that they should give him the benefit of the doubt. If Howard wanted his painting to stay in he had a reason, he's an intelligent artist, a very good artist. Who *is* the other guy to make him take it out? And I asked David Sylvester if he could imagine, in 1890, some men in Paris, intelligent men, organizing a show called 'The Painting of the Eighties' – what did he think would have been in it? I bet you very little of what we think now was the good painting of the eighties, probably no Van Goghs. He'd just died anyway, and even if people had seen one or two of his paintings they probably would have thought they were not very good.

It's still the same now. These people, with all the good will in the world, can't see. In fact, the treatment of late Picasso is a classic example: I think this is what happened, and people will tell me off, but from 1910 to 1950 Picasso dominated serious painting. Anybody who had a serious interest in art knew and looked at Picasso – he was a dominant influence. And, after the war, American painting was probably the first painting that looked as though it was unPicassoesque and yet modern. It was thrilling for people. Thrilling. They thought they were out of this terrible yoke, this dominant thing. It did look as though Jackson Pollock was unPicassoesque. Well, he *is* Picassoesque, actually. His work is from Picasso. It couldn't have happened without him, and his debt is bigger than we think. You can understand why people were thrilled to think they were getting away from this giant. But we haven't got away from him, that's the problem.

I've always complained that the trouble with a lot of modern painting is that it is not interested in the visible world. That simply means that artists must go in on themselves, and their art becomes an internal one. This is okay but it can be merely therapeutic, and then it moves out of the realm of art.

---

* David Sylvester, art historian, writer and critic.

That's the theoretical flaw in it. I'm not suggesting exciting art wasn't produced in that way. There is certainly exciting abstract art, but I think the claims for it were very overdone, especially the idea that the visible world would disappear from art. I do think that is a naive idea. It *cannot* be. The visible world is too interesting and fascinating to us, especially the figure. The figure can't disappear from art. In fact, the only time it disappears from art is when it's proscribed, as in Islamic or Jewish art, which is abstract, highly developed and of great beauty, but one that inevitably becomes ornamental.

I never saw abstract art as 'new'. It's a lot older than 1910! The principles are, certainly – people have known about them for ages. But an art that's not based on looking inevitably becomes repetitious and not that interesting, whereas one that is based on looking finds the world infinitely interesting, and always finds new ways of looking at ourselves. I did get myself involved in a few arguments in the art world over this theory, but I *knew* that painting would deal again with the physical world. Of course, without drawing you get very crude results; you need those skills to accomplish things. It will happen though, there are signs that painting is recovering, taking notice of the physical world once again.

A few years ago there was a crisis when people moved on to conceptual art, and the idea that you could have art without the object. But all that was leading to a dead end. There's always been art without the object: it's called poetry or music. It's always been there. But the idea of being able to make a *visual* art without an object is just crazy! We need depictions. Unfortunately, people were leaving depictions behind because of photography. The depictions that *were* being made used the camera. That's fine, they thought, the camera's dealing with that area now.

Look at what happened a few years ago with what they called 'neo-expressionism'; it seemed then that people wanted to make depictions. But we all want to make depictions: it's a very deep desire and it won't go away. The moment depictions appeared again in painting, then people had to consider Picasso's work. It couldn't be ignored. Of course, the moment it is looked at, it is obvious that it is much more interesting than what we call the new depictions, which are mostly still an old way of seeing.

Unfortunately, according to art history, cubism's influence was on abstraction and not on realism. Realism went its own way, they said, but cubism *was* realism, that's the point. It's all difficult: Picasso made it difficult, but it won't go away, it has to be dealt with. I certainly have to deal with it, and I don't know whether I can, I haven't that kind of talent. Nobody has the kind of talent that Picasso had, never mind the soul! He has opened up things, so that they can be developed, and in that sense his achievement is incredible and unique. But his work is open-ended: it can go on in a way that Mondrian's art, for instance, cannot. Mondrian took his art to a kind of conclusion.

I'm sure that the only way art can be replenished is by going back to nature. You don't just look at Picasso: you look at him and he tells you to go to nature. Nature is infinite. The idea that we've absorbed nature, and painting can go on to something else, seems naive to me now. Of course, a lot of abstract painters never said that; they said: this is about the visible world. At least the abstract expressionists said that, but then in the sixties people did claim otherwise. Frank Stella, for instance, said: it's just what you see there, that's all there is. Essentially, he was saying that there's just this surface, and that's it. But that is taking away what you might call magic in art. I use the word 'magic' because I don't know what else to use, but the magic is there. I've no doubt of that. The magic is the bit you can't quite define.

I think we could be entering a much more fascinating time in art once again. I know there are people who think my claims are ridiculous, and I know those people would love to push me aside, but I also know that they can't quite do that! People are annoyed that it might be more serious than they think. Well, that amuses me, of course. I'm perverse enough to be amused by that. You know, if people ask some kind of dumb question like, 'What's it like to be a successful artist?' I don't know what to say, and so I say that I don't really see myself that way. No artist could see himself that way, really. It's a struggle, it's always a struggle.

PJ: Well, I think it must be more difficult for you because you have been taken up by the media, you are well-known.

DH: That's why it's better for me in L.A., you see. If I was in London I couldn't isolate myself quite the way I can here. There's a constant barrage of 'Would you do a talk on TV?' and I get a bit fed up. I only do it if I've something to say. I think that's the main reason I came back here, apart from the visual stimulus from the surroundings. But you still have to deal with the mechanics of life, everybody has to deal with these, but I've got it quite well organized. Other people do it for me! I'm not an extravagant person, I work most of the time. All I need is space and equipment, and as long as I have that then, frankly, I couldn't give a damn. Although I think the public image is quite different, isn't it?

PJ: It is, yes, but you've cultivated that quite astutely, because you can use that to your advantage, when you need to, but there's always going to be an ambiguity. They will both love you and hate you, and you wanted that. But it also allows you to hide behind it and do your serious work.

DH: I don't really do anything else but work.

PJ: That's clear. Your output is prodigious. And it was clear that you weren't sleeping when you were working on the joiners. I knew you couldn't have slept to have got through that. And somehow it's photography but it's not photography, that's what fascinated me.

DH: Well, I said that; it's not photography because it's to do with drawing, yet it is photography because it's using a camera!

PJ: It's interesting that painting moved away from so-called naturalism at the time when photography was proliferating in that area. Photography has got a lot to answer for in that respect, hasn't it?

DH: Yes. And also it's probably no coincidence that about the same time cubism was being formed, when only a few people had seen it, the movie happened too. Now, the moving picture would appear to be much more radical than the cubist picture – in one way it's more like life, but in another way it's not. The movie is still the same way of seeing. It gives an illusion of movement, but the time experienced is linear. You can't go back with it, you can only pretend to go back, while that wheel is relentlessly going forward. And that fucked up the flow of ideas which now we might be beginning to see . . . But the movie was so exciting, and wonderful things were done with it, so what did it matter? You could make movies in a different way. All attempts at 3D movies or 3D photography are trying to make things more real. They bring the screens right round you. There have been various experiments, and all of them failed because they didn't bring you closer.

The joiners do bring you closer. You could make a much more 3D movie on the same old flat screen using a depiction. All those attempts to bring everything in around you are part of a naive belief that you can re-create the whole world. Well, you can't. Where would you put it? Next to the whole world? I mean, there's no place for it. It's a mad idea. It has to be a depiction, and depictions can be made more vivid with the present technology. They could have been made more vivid fifty years ago. But it takes time to see all these things. They certainly could be made now. You saw that little experiment I did on the TV?

PJ: The *South Bank Show.** Yes, I was going to ask you about that because it seemed to me that you'd started something there that you should go on with.

DH: The thing is, you can't do that on your own, unlike the photographs and the paintings. Well, I have one or two people to help me. But you need a team of people to make the film. I'd be willing to try.

PJ: I think it would be great. But I think Bragg should have repeated your film and perhaps slowed it down . . .

DH: Oh, I told them that. I *said* to them . . .

PJ: They *threw* it away. It must have taken hours to do . . .

DH: Well, it lasted forty-five seconds.

49

PJ: It's crazy. You can't see it in that short time.

DH: I did know it was going to work in a strange way. You were going to see a depth of things that you didn't see on the TV screen. I said that they should simply repeat it, and they complained it would cost too much, so I said: just repeat it on the fucking video. The first person to ring them up after that show was the guy who made the movie *The Draughtsman's Contract*.

PJ: Peter Greenaway.

DH: Yes. He wanted to know how it was done. Well, it seemed to me if you know about films you can tell, really. But then *The Draughtsman's Contract* was about looking through holes, wasn't it?

PJ: It was, as I recall, about passive response to the landscape and it was irritatingly pretentious.

DH: It did have something, although it wasn't a great movie. But having seen his film, I could see why he'd be interested in my ideas. Silly old Melvyn! I said: show it three times,

---

* An edition of the *South Bank Show*, edited and presented by Melvyn Bragg, which dealt with Hockney's increasing preoccupation with photography, was transmitted by London Weekend Television on 13 November 1983. The programme ended with a Hockney experiment 'movie joiner'. He used a 16mm film camera to record a man descending a staircase and sitting down in a chair. The action was repeated nine times for the camera and Hockney chose a different angle of view from which to film on each occasion. Then a frame blow-up was selected from each movie shot and Hockney prepared a rough photocollage from them. When he was happy with the juxtaposition of these, the selected film 'takes' were mixed together optically on to one piece of film. In real time the action only appeared to happen once, but accidental (although wholly desirable) repetition would occur between adjacent frames. This gave the impression that each image carried somehow the 'echo' of another close to it, enhanced by the fact that the repeated action (man down staircase and into chair) was never of exactly the same duration. Although this excursion into film was much admired, Hockney has not continued with any other movie or video experiments.

because the unsophisticated would hardly have noticed anything in that short time, although the very sophisticated might be videoing it anyway, so that they could repeat it for themselves. But there must be many people intelligent enough to perceive that something different was happening, who didn't record it, or didn't have a video. We could have shown it three or four times. It's only forty-five seconds long, and it was interesting. What happened was that I had taken that simple scene of a man coming down the steps, and divided it into nine sections, hand-holding the camera.

PJ: And that's what gave it that slight movement along the edges.

DH: Yes.

PJ: Never a tripod.

DH: No. He had to do it nine times – each take lasts for forty-five seconds long. But you're seeing four-and-a-half minutes of time in forty-five seconds and nothing is speeded up. Consequently you get a feeling of depth. I did that simply; I took all these films, then I said to them: give me a still from each one; and then I patched it together in a particular way. But, if you had one camera with twelve lenses that could somehow merge on a video camera, all feeding back into one thing here …

PJ: Then you'd probably have to have a different focal length on each, wouldn't you, so that each one could come in closer to an object. You'd have to have a sophisticated, multi-lens zoom.

DH: It seems possible to do …

PJ: Yes, technically it's possible.

DH: At least it's not impossible … I mean, there are a lot of technicians and camera factories, aren't there? One of the effects of doing this nine times was that bits of him sat down before other bits. I liked that. I asked them to keep it in. It was as if you'd glanced away and then another bit sat down. The point is to bring *you* into the picture. That's what they are all trying to do. All attempts at 3D are trying to bring you into

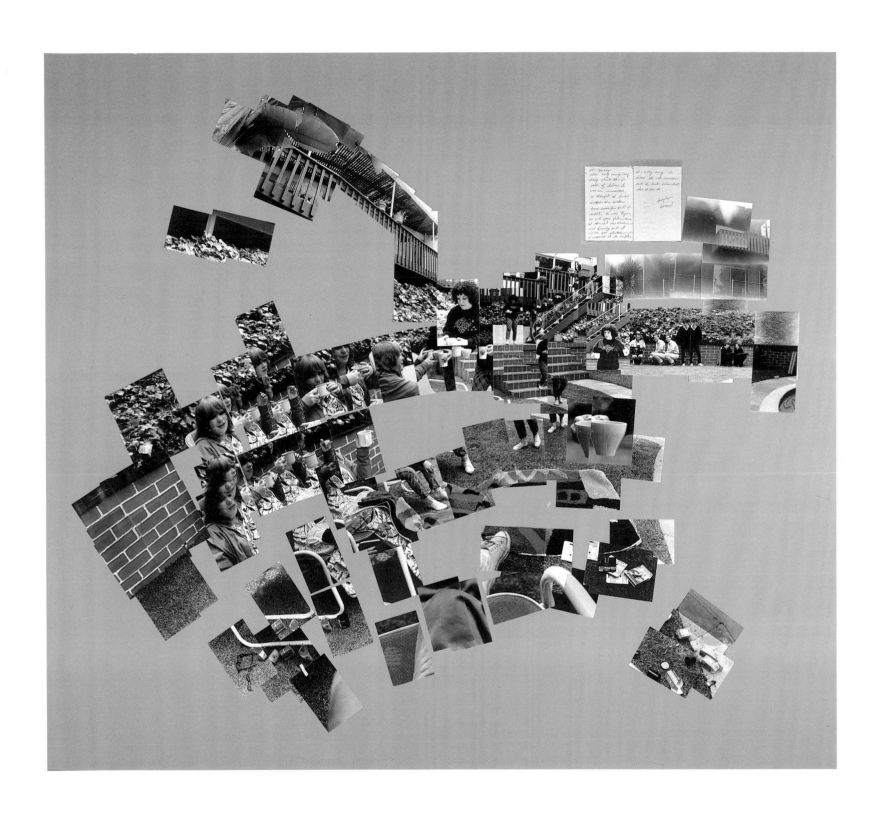

Fredda bringing Ann and Me a Cup of Tea,
April 16th 1983, Los Angeles (photographic collage)

the picture. The Chinese technique of the scroll does take you into the picture: you can wander around in your imagination. On the flat movie screen you need something like this so that the audience could be brought in closer to the viewing. That experiment of mine made action more vivid and gave narrative a much more subtle treatment as well. You must literally make the viewer look all over the screen. He must acknowledge the surface of the screen before he can see beyond it; whereas with conventional perspective the viewer has to pretend the surface isn't there in order to see beyond it. Consequently the single photograph is taking life away from you.

PJ: That's when you end up being overly concerned with the surface, as a film-maker or photographer, attempting always to make it look more beautiful, more true, more this, more that. But the truth is actually beyond the surface.

DH: In order to get the effect with my film, the eye had to look. And it did work, even on that little TV screen. You were forced to move about just as you are with the photographs. Your eye is forced to move about, which gives you a feeling of life again.

PJ: Well, you know John Berger* says that photography is all about death.

DH: There's something in that, in the sense that duration is life, and the photograph has no duration. It is dead in that sense. Never mind about art critics or photography critics, it would be interesting to know what a physiologist or a psychologist thought of those pictures.

PJ: I came out of your exhibitions, particularly the one with the picture of your mother in,† and the one of the yellow guitar, feeling more excited and wanting to go back to life, more so than with any other photographic show I've ever seen. It was full of life, and there's death in every other photograph that I know.

DH: All photographs share the same flaw: lack of time. Painting has never suffered from that. With photography, the way of seeing is one problem, but there are still those chemicals which take away the time so that it is all seen instantly. It does all relate, you know.

PJ: Only for those with the eyes to see!

---

* John Berger, novelist and art critic who has written extensively on photography.
† 'My Mother, Bradford, Yorkshire, 4th May 1982' (see page 61).

On the plane to Mexico City: May 1984

David, who had known Dennis Hopper for twenty years and rightly guessed that his illness would not resolve itself in a couple of weeks, invited me to join him on a visit to Mexico City. The Museo Rufino Tamayo was mounting a retrospective exhibition of theatre designs (organized by the Walker Art Center in Minneapolis and subsequently shown at the Hayward Gallery in London) which also included a room devoted to David's photography. He planned to supervise the reproduction of certain exhibits for the London catalogue and posters, and to experiment within the model of an opera set with his own photography. Our talk on the plane was punctuated by David's ability to cat-nap at a moment's notice.

PJ: The main difference between Picasso and yourself, I think, is that you can lead people who are not artists to see much more clearly, whereas Picasso was dealing with a very esoteric area which needs an artist to decipher it. Your work can be appreciated easily by people who aren't trained artists.

DH: Picasso was seen as a very esoteric artist in the end because what he was doing was revolutionary and difficult. It had to be done in a certain way. Also, he didn't write or talk to people, he was a painter, essentially.

Many people do say to me: oh, you start talking about Picasso, David, and you make it so clear. Well, that's only because they hear me talking with the excitement of an artist, rather than a writer or a scholar. I get excited because I'm absorbing ideas which will eventually come out in my work. I'm so convinced of this way of seeing now: I know it will make things richer for everybody.

PJ: I was looking this morning at the steering wheel photograph,* and it occurred to me that you put space into your later photographic work by not filling every area with images, so the equivalent of the grid of the Polaroid work is actually areas of space which allow the eye to move freely. When you were shooting the later work you used a frame many many times. Do you see from the edges or are you looking straight through that frame at individual details?

DH: I keep both eyes open when I'm shooting. I don't close one eye.

PJ: So you keep an open view and a detailed one. But are you aware of exactly where the frame begins and ends?

DH: Yes, you have to be. In that sense each individual piece relies on composition a great deal. If it wasn't well composed your eye wouldn't go to it. It wouldn't move about.

PJ: So one is accepting a certain convention, perhaps even a fact?

DH: One thing I realized is that you must have the philosophy that everywhere you look is interesting, no matter what it is you see. I do believe that. Seeing is life – that is the thrill, so it doesn't matter *where* you see. You can actually do it anywhere. It's all interesting. It doesn't matter what it is – a bit of carpet, an ashtray, a bit of junk. If you want to go and see my Polaroids, they are all in London. Even though I'd shown them, I didn't want to sell them. I've kept them, every single one, because I didn't know what they were. And I thought if I sell them, you know what the art world is like. Each piece is unique, naturally, so if I say: well, it's three thousand dollars, then I know the year after it'll be eight. That's the art world. So I thought: I don't need the money, although they cost me a great deal to do . I mean, I'd spent a lot of money on film. But the longer I keep them the more they are worth.

---

* 'Steering Wheel, October 1982' (see page 63).

Yellow Guitar Still Life,
Los Angeles, 3rd April 1982
(Polaroid collage)

PJ: Absolutely. Also they constitute a revolutionary body of work.

DH: Oh yes, I know that. With the others, you could make a print and it didn't matter. I kept the negatives. They are all filed away in the proper negative store. but if I let the Polaroids go, that show at the Hayward would have been difficult because I would have had to borrow them. And it's a massive body of work. There's far more in Mexico than there was in the Hayward show. And you can see a development in various ways. But when the critics say: ah, people have done this before, well they can't have done it all before, because I know that each one has been done in a quite different way. I didn't want to repeat things at all. Later, when people showed me what one photographer had done by joining prints together I saw that he'd got only one idea and he simply repeated it. There was no sense of space in his work; it was flat and dead.

PJ: I honestly think that photography is no longer the same after this work of yours. I'm absolutely convinced of that.

DH: *I* know that. It cannot be the same, because so many things have been overcome there. Not just one thing, many

things. Did you see the guitar one? It wasn't shown in England, I don't think, the first one, the cubist one.

PJ: I did. I thought it was very beautiful. I loved the formality, the rigorous way that you put it together. And the colours, too, the yellows of the guitar.

DH: Ah, you saw the yellow one. That's done in artificial light. The one here in Mexico is the second one I did and was done in daylight. It's better, I think, and it took me a long time, it took all day. And I've got all the rejected Polaroids. You know, when you're working you keep altering things, taking something away, re-doing it, making it better. I kept all the rejects.

PJ: Maybe you'll investigate those again one day?

DH: Oh yes, I've no doubt. I said they were rejects but I've carefully put them away in drawers. Perhaps I should have put them in envelopes and written which was which.

PJ: You'll remember.

DH: I've no doubt. In fact, I bet if I started piecing those together now I'd see other things.

David Asleep on the Plane to Mexico City,
photograph by Paul Joyce, May 1984

Mexico City:
May 1984

As the exhibition at the Museo Rufino Tamayo was open all day, we had to work at night between 8 p.m. and dawn on lighting and photographing the exhibits. David, all the while, was making his own 35mm and Polaroid joiners. He also tried to shoot (for the first and last time) a large-format joiner on the photographer's plate camera. The end result was unsatisfactory from David's point of view, and he found the camera itself cumbersome and unfriendly. During these nights I was able to shoot a few pictures of my own of David, usually when he had dropped off to sleep.

The week we spent together in Mexico produced some of our longest and most intense conversations. It is rare to have so much of David's time so freely given. Even at his Los Angeles studio (which is deliberately cut off from the telephone) there seemed to be constant interruptions and demands made on him. But in Mexico he was able to relax. He also became passionately interested in Mexican history, devouring book after book, and visited the museums, spending hours in front of the Diego Rivera murals. A whole day raced by at the Anthropology Museum, which David believes to be one of the wonders of the world.

In Mexico City it soon became clear to me that David was communicating in a quite unusual and concentrated way. I would start each session with a definite set of questions but these would largely go unspoken. He would move from topic to topic with a speed which often left me feeling out of control. I had to go with the current and any attempt to fight the tide was tiring and counter-productive. So these conversations were undirected, but they constitute the heart of this book. We stopped talking only when David was working or sleeping. The pieces of conversation were beginning to fit together like an enormous, philosophical jigsaw puzzle.

Our conversations in Mexico took place at: the Museo Rufino Tamayo; the Anthropology Museum; the Camino Real Hotel; David's suite there and the coffee shop (he avoids bars, being uninterested in alcohol and bored by drink-induced banter); in front of Diego Rivera's murals; at two or three fine restaurants; and in the streets between the hotel and the museum, a walk of some twenty-five minutes during the late evening rush hour and the extreme quietness of dawn.

A model of the opera set for Le Rossignol (some twenty feet across by eight feet high) had been installed at the Museo Rufino Tamayo, and David used this as the basis for various photographic experiments during our Mexican visit. When working on the joiner he walked up and down, examining the model minutely, and then began to photograph it step by step in passing. He first photographed it on a 10 × 8 plate camera, using transparency film. A little later he used his 35mm camera, and constructed a photocollage back in Los Angeles which he called 'Walking Past Le Rossignol, May 1984'. This was the depiction he liked best. The Rossignol work reminded me very much of the Ryoanji Garden photocollage, and I questioned him again about it.

DH: When I took the photograph of the Ryoanji Garden, I knew it would be very different, but I didn't know how it would come out. I'd no idea. And when I was first laying it out I got them all mixed up and I had to have them all printed again so that I could put the pebbles in the right place. Somebody asked if I had just taken one of the pebbles and repeated it, but you'd soon see the repetition and it would stop the time element. The pebbles had to be in the right place for it to work. I had to count and really look at those pebbles to link one with another. I made two photographs to show together, and one was made from one fixed point but looking everywhere. The moment you put the two together you know what that is – it's movement – and you've got a different kind of photograph. There can't be many photographs made of reality without perspective. I doubt whether there have

Walking Past Le Rossignol, April 1984 (photographic collage)

been any, because it would have to be done this way.

PJ: Ryoanji is a very disturbing picture. I visited that garden after I'd seen the picture at the Hayward show and I had great difficulty with it. I knew that it was a special picture when I saw it, but I actually had to visit the garden to appreciate what you'd done!

DH: Your eye is forced to move to every corner of the picture, up and down, because there's a different time in each section. And as your eye moves in time, so does the picture. You can't experience that with an ordinary picture taken from one point. And if you break that one point down, then naturally you get a greater illusion of space because it's all there in your mind. This way of seeing will eventually be used: somebody is going to use it. I thought Steven Spielberg might have been interested, but maybe he hasn't seen this work yet. It is difficult to talk about it theoretically, but once you see it you know it works.

Frankly, I wouldn't have believed this only two years ago. I thought then that only technology would improve the picture. Now I know that it can't. These changes have to begin in the mind: you have to analyse how a picture is depicted. I realize what I'm talking about will be understood only by people who are on the same wavelength. Nevertheless, there's a room with those joiners in here at the museum in Mexico and people didn't just walk through the room, did they? It's not possible to take it all in at a glance. Once your eye gets into the picture, it starts moving about on the surface, which is all it can do, but that surface keeps taking you in, you keep breaking it down. Things have got to move on. What stopped us was the belief that technology was going to change the picture.

My theories may seem intellectual, but they aren't above people. The pictures work for everybody. My mother was very excited about them, and my mother's a sweet, simple soul. There's no doubt that people will realize that they are seeing more. Everybody wants to see more. It's a very natural desire, isn't it? The ideas may be very profound, but the

Walking in the Zen Garden at the Ryoanji Temple, Kyoto, February 21st 1983 (photographic collage)

Standing in the Zen Garden at the Ryoanji Temple, Kyoto, 1983, photograph by Paul Joyce

pictures do lead to a greater reality.

PJ: Can you talk a little bit about memory, the building of memory into images? I think that's one of the things that you opened up, particularly with the Ryoanji Garden pictures.

DH: Well, this is the hardest thing of all to talk about because it's so weird – memory, vision, what we're seeing *now*. And when I say now, I mean at this moment. That moment's now altered because time is flowing all the time – our life is going on. But memory must be part of vision as well, because in that sense everything is now, the past is now. Again, this proves to me that objective vision cannot be, because each of us has a different memory. When you look at this, you remember that you've seen things like it before. Your memory comes in and forms part of it, contradicting the objectivity of vision. I think that garden is one of the most radical of those photocollages because it's a memory picture in a way that an ordinary photograph can't be. It's not possible to see the garden that way. You can only see it in an accumulated way in your memory. If you stop at any one point it doesn't look like that, yet it must look that way in your mind, especially afterwards.

Think of that garden! When I think of the garden I think of my pictures of it, because they were a scrutiny of it. In a way, this is the most interesting aspect of it, because it makes you realize that what and how we're seeing are different for everybody because their memories are different. Again this is what Picasso is about – if he makes a painting of a face showing front and sides, different aspects, it's a memory picture because we can't see these all at once, we see them over a period of time. That's a more truthful way of representing what you see, really. It's like those photographs: they are linked very deeply to Picasso, but I always said that was the source, his questioning of the way of seeing. The most mysterious aspect of it is the hardest to grasp. Do we see after images, do we see before it happens, which sounds absurd and irrational but might not be. Oddly enough, the movie can't quite deal with this because it deals with linear time. You're seeing many pictures that give one illusion, but the pictures are made in the old way of seeing just one thing at a time, and they simply accumulate. The movie and the photo-graph, that way of seeing, may have affected us much more deeply than we think.

PJ: So it's more difficult to change, more difficult to make people see the other possibilities.

DH: Yes, this may be why people lost interest in Picasso. I've noticed I'm more interested in Picasso than I am in the movies. In fact, if I analyse my own reaction to the movies, I loved them when I was young; my father loved them too, and we went two or three times a week. We would see anything, *anything*. Just looking at the moving picture was enough. Imagine what it was like in 1910 when people first saw moving pictures. It must have been thrilling! It's less thrilling to us now because it's all around us, twenty-four hours continuous television. You can see it any time you want. And we accept it as a vivid depiction of reality.

Remember that the movies were started silently, in a totally visual medium. Most movie techniques were worked out by 1928. And then sound was added, and they thought they were making films more real by doing this. Unfortunately, they simply added sound to a form that had been worked out for another way, a visual way, of telling the story.

It's interesting that television is actually the other way around. It began as radio, simply as sound, and then they added pictures to that. In the silent movie you had to fill in the dialogue yourself, although the characters were there in front of you, and you somehow knew what they were saying. The radio play was devised to give you the feeling of what something was like: they worked out a form to tell the stories only with sound. So they have both become polluted mediums, meeting somewhere in the middle. They have not been worked out properly. The first talkies worked so well at the time because they relied heavily on the dialogue: they were witty and enjoyable and clever. But I think now something has happened. Both TV and films are a bit flat – they need expansion.

Of course, there can be more vivid depictions made. There will be in the future, I've no doubt. And this leads you to the central problem of depiction – that it is not an attempt to re-create something, it's an account of *seeing* it. That's what it should be. Cézanne told us that; he wasn't concerned with apples, he was concerned with his perception of apples. That's clear from his work.

When I had all those arguments with Alain Sayag I told him that the main problem with the photograph is to do with time. There is no time in a photograph, I said. So he replied that sometimes it took a long time to take a photograph if you were arranging things. I protested that this didn't count because the time wasn't then in the seeing. That is like the suggestion that the genius of Cézanne depended on how carefully he arranged the apples before he started painting. Of course the important point is not the arranging of the apples! He spent very little time doing that. It's the seeing of them, and his account of his seeing them, that is important. All Cézanne's questions are there in the seeing, and he questioned things all the time. People simply hadn't questioned things before. They accepted the way in which they saw.

Picasso and others then took off from Cézanne, and now I'm trying to take off from Picasso in an even more radical way. Things can become more vivid because they are closer to the truth. I haven't seen anything anybody has written about those photographs which would link them to Cézanne, questioning what's happening when you *see* using a camera. Cézanne would have done this with a camera; in the end he would.

PJ: Would you say that your photographic work is an attempt to make people see things in a different way?

DH: More vividly, I would say. People react because it is more vivid. My work is also a base for future work, for me and for anybody else who wants to use it. There is an advantage in using the camera because people do have certain beliefs about it. In the joiners, if someone appears with six feet, people will know that they have simply seen the pair of

Still Life with Jug and Fruit (detail) by Paul Cézanne

feet three times. That was, of course, true with Picasso's work, but many people couldn't accept it. Again, I realized that, whatever you do, you can't have two heads, you must have one. Even with Picasso, if he puts in two noses, it's the same nose seen twice within one face. I want to deal with the figures: these are the most difficult and with them I come up against Picasso, I have to deal with him there. I'm going to attempt it, though it is hard and I throw a lot away. People do say I'm crazy!

PJ: Do you think the reason why your photographs were so hugely successful, and they were, even for people who would be bored by ordinary photographic exhibitions, is that people recognize that this is the way things are?

DH: There's more truth there, that's all.

PJ: Those joiners have a sense of breath in the body, those portraits of your mother, for instance . . .

DH: That's because your eyes have to move to look at them. There's no way you can see the joiners all at once. It's impossible. Your eyes won't let you. The muscles won't let you. So you get a feeling of life looking at them. Life is given back to you. The moment you start looking you're forced to go on looking, even when you know the photograph.

  Look at that steering wheel picture. You start moving around, you are forced to look at every piece of it: you couldn't do that if the picture weren't clear. If you jumble it up you get a kind of mad jigsaw effect, and your eye is revolted by it – it's not invited in.

  Finally, the joiners are about clarity, which is a quality I'm always striving for. It's something you do have to strive for. Shapes do change when you move: they are fluid really, even though they seem solid.

PJ: The joiners lead you back to a relationship with the world: you start to look again at what's around you rather than merely accepting it. Maybe movies or television are closer to most people's perception. Life is a moving picture that comes through a tube care of somebody else. You gaze through your little frame; it passes and you go to sleep. You

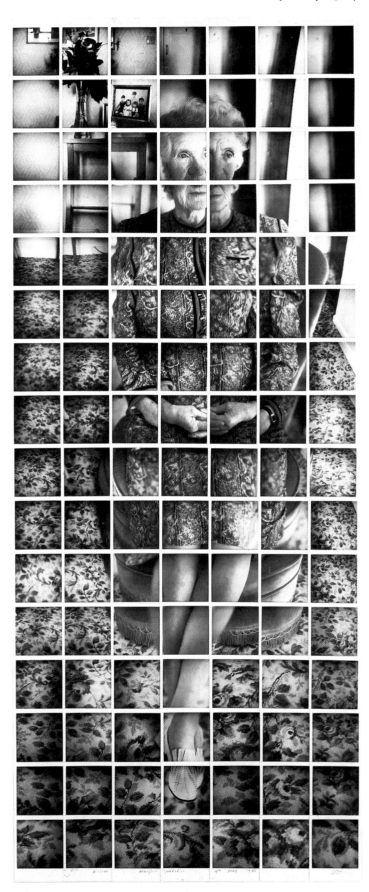

My Mother, Bradford, Yorkshire, 4th May 1982
(Polaroid collage)

Noya & Bill Brandt with self portrait (although they were watching this picture being made) Pembroke studios London 8th May 1982

wake up and there's another little frame. Life, though, shouldn't be like that.

DH: I've no doubt that those photographs I took will make people look at everything in a more interesting way – the little tear on one piece of paper, the shadow on another. But good painting has always done that – made you see things. And the most ordinary can be the most extraordinary.

PJ: Why is it that photography, which, after all, has been around now for a hundred years in a fairly advanced state, hasn't taught us those things?

DH: Well, it's because its way of seeing was fixed. I'm sure of that. I had a lot of conversations with Annie Leibovitz a year ago. She came out and photographed me – she's a very bright girl, and she confessed that my photographs disturbed her, but she thought what she was doing was all right because she was working within the limitations of photography. My photographs had disturbed her because they had extended the limitations, and therefore she was now working under some artificial limitations. She then asked me what she should do? So I said: if I were you, I'd adopt these joiner techniques because they will make things more vivid. And she was frightened of that because she thought it was *my* style. So I said: *I* don't think it is – you do it in another style. But it isn't a style, it's a technique, and different people can use it to express themselves in different ways. But are we going to see it?

PJ: Well, I think we're going to see it first from you. Your style won't change, but I think that your interests will, and that will be reflected in new work. What worries me about photography is that people can produce almost exactly similar images, and it's very often impossible to tell who has taken a particular photograph. Then you get someone like Annie Leibovitz who paints Meryl Streep with a clown's make-up and has her holding her cheek in order to make it a different image. And Leibovitz's images are stamped with a meretricious surface concern which becomes her style.

DH: Well, it's because she thinks that the only thing she can

Steering Wheel, October 1982 (photographic collage)

do is alter the subject matter, because she can't alter the seeing of it. I'm suggesting that the subject matter is less important. It's the way it's seen that's more important. That's like suggesting that Cézanne wasn't any good because those apples weren't any good. They were cheap apples. Why didn't he buy the better quality ones?

PJ: Exactly. Cézanne wouldn't make the real apples redder, or greener, in order to see those apples redder or greener in his oil or watercolour. Leibovitz, and I don't mean this to be an attack on her particularly, we just happen to be talking about her, feels it necessary to paint something, to make something up in order to capture its essence. All she does is create a different surface.

DH: It's cosmetic really, what she's doing. I told her that. She hated me saying that. And when we got out to the desert she'd taken all these lights as if *they* were making that picture.

PJ: And your picture is so much more interesting than hers – a story is told. Hers is just a flash picture taken in the middle of nowhere, and with all that equipment and everything.

Noya and Bill Brandt with self-portrait,
Pembroke Studios, London, 8th May 1982
(Polaroid collage)

Photographing Annie Leibovitz while She Photographs Me,
Mojave Desert, February 1983
(photographic collage)

DH: Well, that's why I made my picture. It was mocking it, obviously mocking it. And it was made with the camera that happened to be in my pocket.

PJ: It seems to me that the polarity between your two approaches couldn't be better delineated than that!

DH: And sticking the joiner together I asked her: could you give me one of yours and I'll stick that on as well? But she

A Member of the Wardens' Service fitting a Gas Mask, colour photograph by John Hinde *c.* 1944

understood, when I showed it to her. She said: you've got the picture. She's not a dummy at all.

PJ: But she's trapped by the medium.

DH: Oh, yes, but she's very aware of that.

PJ: But most photographers *are* trapped by the medium, that's why it needs an artist to come along and throw the restraints to one side.

DH: And in the end you realize that only an artist can do that; in a way, that's his job.

PJ: All the best photographs I've seen have been taken by artists, not photographers – Humphrey Jennings, Paul Nash, John Piper, Henry Moore, for instance.

DH: I would have thought any good artist would be able to take interesting photographs.

[After an interval]

PJ: It seems to me that photography has two great strengths – anthropology and sociology – and by their choice of subjects the best photographers acknowledge this instinctively.

DH: I have here a book about people working during the war.* Although the people are clearly posed, their faces are extraordinarily good. It took me a while before I realized what it was that was so good. It was something you couldn't fake because the book was made during the war, and the faces

---

* *Citizens in War – and After* by Stephen Spender with colour photographs by John Hinde (George Harrap Ltd, 1945). This book was an examination of the Civil Defence Services which operated during wartime. Spender's objective was to discover in what ways people behaved with greater 'social responsibility' in war than they did in peacetime. The book is, in effect, a medley of detail and impressions – part information, part diary, part straight journalism. What makes it particularly interesting to look at now is the quality of Hinde's photographs. There is a directness and immediacy about them, partly to do with the fact that they are all in colour (probably shot on early Kodachrome stock) and partly because these *were* the faces of those fighting the war at home.

A Professional Fireman, black and white reproduction
from a colour photograph by John Hinde *c.* 1944

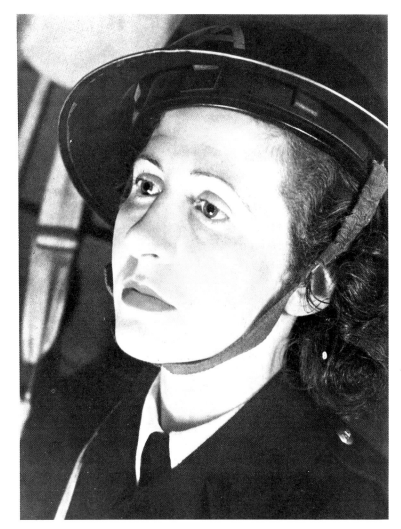

An Ambulance Attendant, black and white reproduction
from a colour photograph by John Hinde *c.* 1944

could not but show that people were worried. You couldn't
re-do them now because people would not have that look in
their eyes, that expression on their faces. But the book was
simply made as a document to show what everybody was
doing during the war. It has that earnestness about it. The
people weren't models, they were real firemen, real porters,
real miners and so on. You can read in their faces that it must
have been a pretty bad time. Even when they were trying to
relax, their faces would show anguish.

If you were filming now, say, making a movie of the Blitz in
London, you would never get faces in a crowd to show real
anguish and concern. I asked Stephen [Spender] about the
photographer because I'd never heard of him. Many photographs were taken in the war by many famous photographers,
but these are very special. The photographer may have been
known at the time but his work is not well-known now, in the
way that, say, Bill Brandt's work is. I'm beginning to think
that photography has fashions about it, even from the past:
Atget, for instance. Berenice Abbot discovered Atget and then
somebody else discovered Lartigue. And there's probably a
vast amount of work out there, a lot of which was not made
as art but might *become* art, just as other things from the past
were not made as art. We see them as art now only because
we are peculiarly self-conscious about art.

PJ: And, presumably, that book was made as a document of that time. I wonder if photography isn't best suited to documentation, and I'm reminded here of August Sander's best work – those marvellous portraits which pinpoint a particular historical period.

DH: And he didn't really make it as art; he wasn't concerned with art, he was concerned with documenting types of people in this period, wasn't he?

PJ: That's right. And he'd stand them against their own background, or against a neutral background – they would just be themselves.

DH: There are probably hundreds of photographs like that from the past.

PJ: Well, I'm not sure. Not with such a rigorous approach as Sander's.

DH: I bet there are, because there must have been millions of photographs taken, millions. And many odd people might have taken them and put them away in some attic.

PJ: Don't you think, even though we've been highly critical of photography, that the photographers who have made it have really dedicated themselves to that medium. Edward Weston dedicated himself, and Sander and Atget did, too.

DH: The only other interesting photographers at all were painters.

PJ: Yes, and I think sooner or later Atget's collection would have been discovered because he was selling prints to museums, they were in artists' collections, and the V & A were sitting on a whole heap of them, they were languishing in some basement.

DH: As soon as the art galleries started dealing in photography the prices went crazy. With Walker Evans, no matter what they were selling for in the galleries, you could write to Washington and buy a Walker Evans photograph for ten dollars.

PJ: I think you still can. I ordered six and paid twenty dollars.

DH: Yes, and they are made from the negatives, and just treated as photographs.

PJ: The same is true of Bill Brandt's photographs in the Hulton Picture Library. You could buy a print from the original negative for a fiver, which makes a nonsense of the photographer paying a printer and saying: this print's all right, then signing it – and charging five hundred pounds.

DH: I loved that when I found out. I suppose if some care is taken in the printing, all right, you're paying for it; but that's an artisan's job, really, not an artist's. It's not a drawing.

PJ: This is where we get to the crux really, between art and photography. Is the moment when an artist chooses, frames and takes that picture a work of art, or is it just a well-seen view? How do we answer that?

DH: One point to be made, of course, is that not all oil paintings are art, are they? That's what you have to remember.

PJ: But some are! What about photographs? Can we say that Walker Evans at his peak, or Sander at his peak, or Atget at his peak were working as artists?

DH: In what they were doing you must say they were artists. The problem is it's still not like drawing or painting, is it?

PJ: They are artists, yes, but maybe it's the *body* of work rather than individual pictures that's important. So Walker Evans's FSA photographs* constitute a body of work. And there was a photograph, which I looked at and admired, of severe irrigation problems in a desert landscape, of a land washed away by water – a very beautiful image, very interesting, very uncharacteristic. He didn't take *that* as an art object, as an art view. He took it to demonstrate erosion by water of

---

* The Farm Security Administration was a US Government unit set up in 1935 employing many of the great American photographers, including Walker Evans, Dorothea Lange, and Ben Shahn. Its objective was to document the plight of the rural poor, mainly migrant farm workers, and to alert people to the dangers of improper land cultivation.

a desert landscape. Now, if that went up for sale in an auction it would probably fetch three or four thousand pounds. But it's simply part of the FSA work he was doing.

DH: It could be that they are not good enough as documents, but they are good enough as art.

PJ: But those pictures seem to me to be much more successful as documents. Isn't it rather that people want to make the mark, they need to have artists working in that medium, so they have to find people to fulfil that function. Photography is an art, so we must find the artist. And, having found him or her we then say we'll show the pictures and they are going to cost you two thousand pounds a print. Look what happened to Diane Arbus. Because she died young and didn't do many prints, they hit the roof. Twenty thousand dollars an original Arbus print, or whatever! Alternatively somebody else makes the print and it's two hundred and fifty dollars. Is the hand of the artist important in photography? Maybe we do want to see photography as art. The people, photographers, and those dealing with it want to elevate it to a higher position than it's due.

DH: The thing is that time sorts it all out really. Time sorts out oil paintings, it sorts out what is art and what isn't. So it's probably folly to try and judge it all now. I mean, some things clearly are art straight away in the sense that all Picasso's marks are art. There's no doubt at all.

Photography will have to wait. It's only a hundred years old. It's not that long when you think that pictures have been made for ten thousand years. It's not arrogant to suggest that. When I said the camera might have been used wrongly for a hundred years, people said it was outrageous, but it isn't actually. A hundred years is not that much in the history of images, is it?

PJ: You know what Walter Benjamin said about the question 'Is photography art?' He said that it was no longer an appropriate question because photography changed the nature of art. And I always thought that was rather good.

DH: I've read his essay, 'The work of art in the age of

mechanical reproduction', and I don't actually agree with it. In fact my little essay for 'The Artist's Eye' was taking an opposite view. Mechanical reproduction is not as mechanical as we think, that's the flaw in his argument. The printer who puts more love into it will do a better job. It's not just the machines, it's somebody caring. And it's still like that. What he misjudged was that mechanical reproduction hadn't been going that long. After all, he wrote in the thirties, and it had only been going for thirty or forty years. It's certainly developed a great deal since then, and, no doubt, it will get better still with new machines and things. But people invent new machines because they *think* they can make it better, which is a subjective judgment in a way. So it's not as mechanical as we think.

I bought the reproduction of Van Gogh's chair – the one in the Tate Gallery – for a pound in Leicester Square and you *can* buy it so cheaply because they've obviously printed thousands of them. It's a very, very good reproduction, and you can see the paint with all its lumps – the illusion of depth in the photograph is about half an inch which is very good indeed. With a bit of side-lighting you get this in the reproduction. I also have a Van Gogh book in which all the pictures must have been re-photographed for the book with a little side-lighting. You wouldn't have got that in the thirties. You might have got a Van Gogh reproduced, even in colour, but it wouldn't have looked that way. Well, what made it look better? Somebody cared; somebody wanted to do it better. You can use machines, but it isn't merely mechanical, you can't say that.

PJ: That's why some books have such a wonderful presence to them, don't they?

DH: And even in the printing of a photograph with the same equipment, one person will do it better than another because they care that little bit more, and put love into it. The source of creativity is love, the source of *all* creativity. A really mechanical age would be inhuman. We wouldn't want it. It's just a science fiction horror. I like to think that!

PJ: When the printer is spending the time and the effort and the attention to get that reproduction right his hands are what are doing it, so you're back again to the hand, aren't you?

DH: Oh, never underestimate the hand. In the seventies a lot of what I would now dismiss as very foolish art underestimated the hand. I went to see Gilbert and George at Christmas, and I had an argument about the hand. I said: the hand is far more important than I ever thought. They said: we don't like the hand; we don't care about the hand. I think they are stupid, actually. I don't care for their art.

PJ: Well, I don't think it *is* art, frankly.

DH: I think their art suffers from all the same problems as photography. These things might work for other people but they can't work for me *now*. Because once you begin to see

the problems you see them all the time. When I had the argument with Gilbert and George they thought I was talking a lot of rubbish. I'm convinced about that. They told people I'd gone bonkers.

PJ: But I don't think their use of photography is interesting either as art or photography.

DH: Without the hand we wouldn't have been able to do anything at all.

PJ: And it's apparently this – the thumb-finger relationship – that's vital, because without the thumb you can't do anything. Isn't that how they check the development of children?

DH: Yes, think of your life if you didn't have the hands. Far

Atlanta, Georgia, 1936 by Walker Evans

worse than being without feet. The hands and eyes are the two elements that the Chinese are concerned about in their paintings. When the eye, the hand and the heart come together, that's when you get the greatest art. I think that's profoundly true. And the eye links to the hand, and the heart gives the love – that's where the creativity comes from, the heart.

PJ: It's a wonderful concept. And there's a lesson there too, because one should only try to represent what deeply moves one; anything else is playing with surface and decoration. You were saying that love is the most important thing. I think that there is also an intense desire to communicate at a non-verbal level.

DH: Why is that intense desire there? Love. Why do you want to communicate? To express the joy of life, of living, however

bad it is. This is the paradox of art as well, that by its nature it must be optimistic in wanting to communicate. The fact that it can happen is in itself a joy. The message might be that we're terrible, but it's the start to make us better, isn't it? That's the paradox of art, in a sense. It's why, in the end, angst works only for a while. But an art that's saying everything's terrible, everything's awful, can't really exist: it's a contradiction of the fact that *some* communication is taking place.

PJ: Do you ever think about your audience, the people who will maybe own or see the pictures? It may be love for the thing that you want to represent, but it's also love for an unknown mass of people, or an individual.

DH: Well, I don't think of them that much. I know that the vast amount of people who know my work know it only

through photography, through reproductions. And it works through reproduction on one level, and that's nice; people respond, and it must mean that there's something there. With really junky art people respond to it for a little bit, but they don't respond fully. Nobody does. In the end, really good art is what people respond to. The definition of whether something's really popular is when it's popular from one generation to the next. There are things that just affect a moment, whereas the genuinely popular, like the Laurel and Hardy movies, Celia [Clark]'s children will laugh at still. They touch universal things, and they are truthful about people. They must be, otherwise children wouldn't be laughing. The only kind of people who don't like Laurel and Hardy must be dull bores. They touch something universal in a very profound way. The Laurel and Hardy films never got Oscars, yet they are going to live longer than a great deal of stuff that was taken much more seriously.

PJ: But do you think they considered their audience?

DH: I don't know whether they did, but they genuinely touch their audiences. My father loved Laurel and Hardy. I think he identified with Stanley, and Stanley's the English one. The fact that they always fail at everything is so human, although the paradox was that they succeeded with their films. Have you seen the one where they are borrowing money from the bank, and the banker says: what is your business? Stanley replies: we're in the restaurant business, so the banker says: where is your business? He replies: why, it's just across the street. And the banker looks out of the window and there's a big sign saying 'Hotel and Restaurant'. But the camera moves out of the window, down the street to a little peanut stand which you know is theirs. I laugh even now and I've seen it so many times. You can't *not* laugh...

In May and June 1981 David Hockney, Stephen Spender and Gregory Evans travelled together to China. The resulting book, written by Spender and illustrated by Hockney, was published as China Diary *by Thames and Hudson in 1982.*

DH: When I went to China I only took the little Pentax 110 with me. I didn't really want to take a camera because I knew that without one I would have to draw everything. I knew we would be moving around a lot and that I would have to devise a method of sketching very quickly. Well, we were moving so fast that even that became almost impossible, so I changed from drawing in front of something to drawing from memory. That's the Chinese way, in any case! And then I did start taking photographs because there were too many things to see.

I noticed that if I did go to a place to photograph (and there were very few occasions I did that) I never saw the place properly because I was always looking through the camera. I was looking, as it were, for compositions, and I hated the idea of that. It's very unpainterly: a painter does not see things like that, whereas the photographer is constantly putting his hand to his eyes, cutting out things, thinking he's isolating things. A painter may isolate things, but he doesn't cut them out in the same way. A painter may work on a rectangle, but the edge of his rectangle can be anywhere he wants. China was the last place I photographed that way: I would never do it again.

This is partly the reason why I tend not to travel around so much now. In Japan I was doing a lot of photography, but it was of a completely different kind. I photographed what I thought were quite ordinary things. They might not look ordinary to people now, but I went to a paper conference, I was staying in a Japanese inn, I travelled on a train: so I photographed the tourist sights just as any tourist would do. The photographs are very ordinary, in a real sense. However, my drawing, or note-taking, is done in a different way, in a much more interesting way. I've always carried notebooks around, but now I'm drawing differently in them. I don't draw simply what is in front of me: I take in everything around. I've become much more aware of my surroundings. And this is what will happen to everyone else. People will suddenly see the whole room, instead of noticing one or two things in it. Wide-angle lenses will therefore become obsolete because everyone will be able to see everything they want to. They will put whatever they want in their pictures.

Tian An Men Square, Peking
(with buses and bicycles) China 1981 (water-colour)

PJ: Do you think photography was adopted for a while by the art establishment simply to make them rich?

DH: There was a period in the seventies when a few galleries began to show photographs as if they were works of art. At that time Ileana Sonnabend, for instance, started publishing prints. It was partly because the photograph was being used in conceptual art to show the documentary side of things. But also there was a craving for images. The intellectual corruption is a complicated issue, but generally there was a belief that an art that was representational was inferior. Somehow people believed there had been a progress which meant we'd moved on from mere representation to a truer definition of art. The idea seemed naive to me. Their theory suggested we had no more to learn from looking at nature than simply seeing what the process of looking was like. It *couldn't* be true.

The problem was that the people who had suggested this theory were treated very seriously, very seriously indeed, by a small group. I'm not suggesting it was a mass of people, or even a few serious people from other areas. A philosopher, for instance, I've no doubt, wouldn't have agreed with this at all.

At the time, the photograph was accepted unquestioningly. People believed the camera to be a machine for recording an objective truth. But what I did with the camera made it a lot less mechanical. We tend to jump to conclusions about what is happening at any moment, but as soon as we begin to look into things more deeply we find we have not necessarily arrived at the right conclusions. What we call the art world, which I happen to know because I'm involved in it, reflected a lot of these wrong conclusions. Naturally it would. And these are only just being questioned now. But the art world was caught. It's a bit of a false world; it's not even what it sounds like. We talk about 'the art world' but they are not actually a bunch of artists, simply people who seem to be respected for their views on art. There are even some artists who respect them. I never did. No theoretician, no writer on art, however interesting he or she might be, could be as interesting as Picasso. A good writer on art may give you an insight to Picasso, but, after all, Picasso was there first. The art world

gathered a momentum of its own and became a kind of modern academy, which had to crack sooner or later because it wasn't built on anything really solid. And it cracked in a way that people didn't really expect.

I don't know whether you remember, but there was a lot of talk about the death of painting, which I never took very seriously. There's something wrong with that argument; it doesn't hold up, and the moment you look into the idea it seems to collapse. It might look as though there's a good deal of junk painting around, but that's probably always been the case. Our view of the past is edited, we tend to see what's good from the past and all the junk simply disappears. We tolerate our own junk, but the future will keep only what was good from now. I think the art world tied themselves up in knots without realizing it.

We are forced to make depictions. They have been made for ten thousand years now, and they are certainly not going to stop. There's a deep, deep desire within us that makes us want to do it. Every depiction was made by means of painting and drawing until the middle of the nineteenth century. The hand made them all until it looked as if the hand was stopping and then they were made by machinery. Now we're getting to the core – it looked as if the hand was disappearing, but, of course, it can't disappear, even from making the depiction. Because the photograph looked like a mechanical depiction, and seemed to confirm previous theories about perspective, the cry was 'From today painting is dead!' – a misunderstanding of what painting was. Painting, after all, realist painting, had been based on the ideas that had made the camera. That's the point. That's the point you mustn't miss. And that's the point that Susan Sontag* does not deal with in her book – the fact that the invention of the chemical process was simply added to a Renaissance drawing machine. The moment you made the chemical process and added to it, I think then you should have *seen* in a different way with it.

---

* Susan Sontag (b. 1933), American critic whose writings include *On Photography* and a collection of essays, *Under the Sign of Saturn*, incorporating a critique of the German writer, Walter Benjamin.

Walter Benjamin to suggest that we were in a mechanical age. My work suggests we're not, even though it might seem that way. This criticism goes beyond art into other areas of life, that's what makes this idea more and more interesting.

PJ: I think your photography has taken you through conventional notions that we know – framing and depiction – back through painting to a discussion about philosophy and to the essential elements of our own lives.

DH: And it becomes a very important subject again, doesn't it? It makes painting important.

PJ: Why is it that the great artist has always been considered as some sort of prophet?

DH: They were in the past, weren't they? I became aware a year ago that it made painting far more important than even I thought up to then. I'd always thought painting was worth while, that it was necessary. The people who had suggested it was dead had accepted too readily the mechanical instruments of depiction, as though they were fixed in that way. That was the flaw in the argument, essentially. But that flaw couldn't be pointed out theoretically. How could you argue it? It had to be pointed out practically. I even had to point it out to myself – to convince myself. And following the thought through was very exciting, just following an instinct that what they were saying couldn't be true. And what started this off was the realization that the photograph wasn't essentially good enough. It couldn't compete with the great painting from the past. Nobody had been able to make a photograph that *moved* you in the way that a Rembrandt did. Nobody had been able to make a photograph that was as exciting as most of the art from the past. After a hundred years it had not happened. Well, I know it's strong criticism!

PJ: You obviously want to talk, and made those connections, but I'm afraid – and I might be the exception – that you're doomed to a dialogue with yourself.

DH: Oh, I'm aware of that now, yes. And it's simply because you can't expect somebody else to be following your mind. On the other hand, if you don't talk to someone you get the

Self Portrait 1640 by Rembrandt

That is my criticism. For a hundred years nobody used the camera properly. They were simply using it in the way Canaletto would.

With my work you can have photographs using chemical inventions to bring the hand in. The joiners bring the hand back. There's no way you can start joining pictures together mechanically, and the more complicated the photography is, the more subtle the hand work becomes. This is true of film, but it can be true of other things as well. The problem is that those mechanical ways dominated, giving us the feeling that the age had become mechanical: the same illusion prompted

most frightening feeling of isolation. You *want* contact with people who are interested in it. People have found me – you found me. In a way that's no accident. When it happens it's because our wavelengths are similar. But it happens in all aspects of life – it's no accident who your friends are. It might appear to be so – that you just happened to meet there, but you meet all kinds of people who you don't bother meeting again, don't you?

PJ: At a certain moment one is hungry for something and then, of course, you leap forward because there's a new world! But that happens very rarely in life. You've made that connection – Picasso is dead, but he's alive for you, and that's your connection. We all need that.

DH: Yes, we all need it. Nobody can work in total isolation. Picasso's last twenty years were a dialogue with himself. There was nobody near him at all. Matisse had died but you can't *actually* compare them. I do think they were different kinds of artists. Matisse was certainly a great artist, a wonderful artist, people knew that. I'm sure Picasso and Matisse, although I don't think they spoke to each other for fifty years, were aware of each other's qualities. There are stories of how, when they met, they started a niggling criticism, but they must have admired each other, must have known that they were both of a very high calibre. There was one story that Picasso said Matisse had painted a blue nude, but she had a pink shape, something like that. But I've no doubt that his last twenty years were absolutely a conversation with himself. There would be people who would be following it, I'm sure, but they would never quite catch up. They couldn't. There was a huge mind there, a different level, a magical level when you begin to grasp it, but we're all a bit behind him. We'll catch up eventually and things will become clearer. The process must start, though, with some other artist seeing it. Only other artists see it, and if it's going to be influential, it has to be through them, not through anybody else. Now I'm gathering momentum back into the painting, so that point is coming soon where I will wish to cut myself off, and I'll just do that. There comes a point where, as Henry Geldzahler* said, 'You just want to be a little artist whistling down the road of life with a few credit cards in your pocket. That's all you want, David, so long as nobody disturbs your work, you couldn't care less.' But as you go on in life you suddenly have to face up to responsibilities – they catch up with you. So I deal with them because, basically, I'm a responsible person. But even though I'm selfish about my work, naturally, as artists are, there are loads of people who I've put off – the kinds of journalists who make you into a celebrity, for instance. They are just a bore. And you know that they just make a lot more trouble for you.

On the other hand, I'm terrified of cutting myself off completely from people who are interesting. But I always think, in the end, that the people who are really interested in your ideas will find you. Like John Dexter.† I'd never met him, but he wrote a letter that was interesting enough for me to write back. It's a terrifying dilemma: if you cut yourself off completely, you're cutting yourself off from life, or the things that keep you going. And it gets harder.

PJ: Is that something to do with being successful, or is it something to do with getting older?

DH: Something to do with getting old, yes, but it's also simply that as you get older, more and more people become aware of your work, that's all. An awful lot of artists who are quite famous within the art world are unknown outside it, and the amount of artists who break out of that is very small. And they must break out for some reason. There must be something in the work that demands it. Picasso is a much more famous artist that Kandinsky, for instance. You put on a Picasso show and millions of people will go to it, but you wouldn't get that number for Kandinsky. Nevertheless, Kandinsky's an interesting artist, and, within the art world, a very famous one. Picasso affects people, his work does get to people. And I've no doubt at all that he'll become a more and more popular artist, like Rembrandt did. His work is not that difficult, it's deeply human, and that's why a million people

---

* Henry Geldzahler, curator, historian and author.
† John Dexter, director of plays, operas and films, and Production Adviser, Metropolitan Opera, New York.

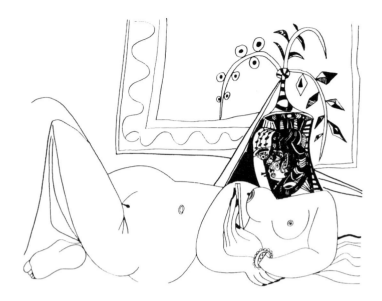

Reclining Nude, Mougins, October 10th 1969
pencil drawing by Pablo Picasso

go. I mean, you wouldn't have a million going to Andrew Wyeth. They might describe him as a popular artist but his art is a peculiarly American-regional thing, isn't it? Picasso's is not. He touches universal things. But after the war he had to isolate himself because he needed his own time. His wife started sorting it out – she became a kind of terror to some people.

PJ: Picasso, though, in his time, was a media personality – he moved from country to country but everybody knew him. He isolated himself. You're the same. I mean, everybody knows you within Western artistic circles, and you're very well-known now in Japan, probably in China, and it looks like in Mexico at the moment too! But you said there must be a reason – if somebody does have that appeal – it's obviously the work, but there's another quality. Now what is that? With you it was up front very early, wasn't it? With gold suits and so on.

DH: Yes, but it isn't just hype ... Do you remember when Elvis Presley died, *The Times* ran an editorial arguing that it had all been an invention of Colonel Parker's plus a lot of hype. Even I was going to write a letter saying that it couldn't

be, but other people wrote saying that Elvis was too big: you can make a hype of something, but he was too big to be put down to hype alone. There was something real there, whether you cared for the music or not, there was something that hit people. And what it was exactly I can't say, but think of all the hyped-up pop singers that have been forgotten. Hundreds of them. And Elvis is not one of them. He touched something. The hype might have helped get him known, but it was the work itself that made him.

He was probably a very outgoing type. I know I am. I like talking to people, but there's another side. You know you have to isolate yourself, you know you have to do all the work on your own. It's lonely. I'm very aware myself at times how deeply lonely I can get, and how difficult relationships are because of what I'm doing. So there are moments when you try and overcome this and try and find somebody to talk to, some sympathetic person. On the whole the world I live in is rather small. I'm not actually a very sociable person, I hate going to big parties. I'd much rather go to dinner with five or six people than thirty. You can't talk to thirty people! Most of the friends I've had I've still got. I still see them. Very few people have gone out of my life; they sort of stay there. I think there's a good reason for that. Somebody pointed out that in my first album of photographs there are the same people as in the latest album twenty years on. They are there still!

PJ: I think it's wonderful that you can see new things, with Celia, and all the people that you draw again and again. It's almost as if you have to look at something familiar in order to see some change.

DH: Well, I always used to joke about Claude Bernard who used to give parties for three hundred of his intimate friends. Nobody can have three hundred intimate friends. How many people in the end can you know that you care about? It's always a small number of friends. You know that there are people who want to come into your world, but you build up a resistance to people. You meet all types of people, awkward buggers, and all sorts. You set up a resistance to some and choose others – it's instinct, isn't it?

[After an interval]

DH: What we call art all starts about the fifteenth century. There were paintings before that but they were parts of bigger things. What we know of easel-painting begins about the late fifteenth century with the invention of perspective and the development of the camera obscura.

PJ: Do you think the camera obscura and easel-painting, and the picture produced from that, has something to do with the question of ownership, something that you can actually carry to a studio?

DH: Well, this is John Berger's stuff, isn't it? I don't go into that side of it, that's the social side. Maybe my viewpoint of the world is too narrow. John Berger's gone into that idea of ownership, but he hasn't linked all the ideas together. On the other hand, the Chinese scroll is very private – the only thing against it is that it can only be viewed by two or three people at a time, whereas an easel-painting can be viewed by many. I know some people say that the different aspects of art all unite, but usually the people who say that are people who specialize in the social problem. You could also say that the way of seeing is a social area – that we are liberators, and this liberation affects other things. But this side of art really affects the social historian and I'm more excited by the new possibilities – that seems to be my job, and the social historian is not going to make paintings. That sounds as if I'm dividing up activity a bit, but I'm not a Renaissance man. I work by instinct, intuition, and follow my passions – that's what I've always done.

PJ: For Renaissance man the perspective that you're questioning now was precisely that sort of revelation.

DH: Oh yes, that's the connection. When it happened they must have been deeply excited and thrilled because pictures changed.

PJ: It's taken a long time for that to be seriously questioned. And you would say, I guess, that photography has unnaturally extended that.

DH: Yes. That's only recently dawned on me, that photography is the Renaissance picture extended, at a point when cubism really was breaking it up. And if photography hadn't been there, cubism would have broken it up more easily. Many more people would have sensed it. But photography extended it. That's why I say that photography is the end. It's the final version of the Renaissance picture and it's time to move on. A new way has already been seen, it has been laid out somewhat primitively. And the more I think about it the more excited I get, but I don't think the art world sees it that way. Of course, there's no reason that they should until it has been properly displayed. That's why, in the end, I'll have to stop giving the lectures and shut myself up there in order to do the work. You have to isolate yourself with a bit of peace and quiet.

PJ: Although the photographs speak directly to more people, I think the paintings have much more effect.

DH: And, because of the photographs, people will begin to understand the paintings straight away. They won't be as difficult as they would have been without the photographs. Just as I think the photographs will make cubism a lot more interesting. More people will look at them carefully. But, actually, going back to cubism to some people is going forward. They haven't got there yet because they haven't understood it. It is a strange thing, but it was partly the moving picture coming along that made the cubist idea look as if it was simply a kind of intellectual painting. The movie appeared to be the most vivid depiction of life yet made, and in a sense it was, but it simply covered up these problems for a while. They will re-emerge. The movie was so exciting that it delayed things for a number of years. It's true, even now, a lot of movie people think films can't be changed. Although I think there are some people interested in doing it – obviously Fellini is, he knows that it's not just a technical innovation, and that it opens up far more possibilities for narrative. People have tried some odd things. There's nothing more boring than an abstract movie – did you ever see any of those 'Scratches on Film'?* Ten minutes of that and everybody is

---

* A loose term for an animation technique where lines and images are etched directly on to motion picture film which is then projected.

The Annunciation with St Emidius
by Carlo Crivelli,

bored to death. The novel keeps being expanded, doesn't it? The methods there are not technological, even though they might be technical ideas. There are cubist novels, James Joyce has written a cubist novel, and even if people don't read his particular work, his influence has filtered down.

[After an interval]

PJ: There's something about photography which is deeply dissatisfying. And I've been struggling to pinpoint just what that is.

DH: I think you *must* feel that before you get deeply interested in what is going on here. There are people, after all, who don't feel that, who think photography is perfectly all right. But for the people who *think*, the ideas will click. A start has been made, at least. The last two years have been an intense time of work and, apart from convincing myself, I certainly convinced a few other people as well. The mass of people who do see my photography just see something more vivid. They don't understand the full implications, which go way beyond pure photography and way beyond art, into all aspects of life itself. And I don't think that will be seen for some time. One aspect of photography is that it's popular, whereas painting is not that popular an art, and probably never was. A certain cultivation is needed to be able to read painting to derive real enjoyment from it. But photography is different – the number of amateur photographers around runs into millions, doesn't it?

PJ: Second only to fishing!

DH: Is it? God, I would have thought it would have surpassed fishing!

PJ: Throughout the world, maybe yes, but in the UK fishing comes first, photography is number two.

DH: Why *is* that? I don't know about fishing, but the urge to depict, the urge to deal with images, is a deep urge. We all have to have depictions of some kind.

PJ: But most people are very happy with their photographs, their albums.

DH: They were. But they might not be now. When you get back to England keep reading the popular photographic magazines ... follow them because that's where you'll begin to see things. If things happen there, then it will show. One piece I read was very intelligent – the guy had done some thinking and he did realize that you can do things completely differently. And he was saying that to the readers. The amateur market is the area where people might be least resistant. You might be amazed, but that's reflective of the amateur. Yes, I know most of those magazines are not up to much. I flip through them once in a while and think there's nothing interesting at all, but it's worth keeping an eye on them. Try it and see. What might happen is that the people who regard themselves as the most serious might be those who are most resistant to any change. That happened in painting – a lot of the resistors regarded themselves as deeply serious and committed people, yet they were the ones who attacked a lot of modern art, saying it was rubbish. So you might well find that amateurs are quite receptive. Painting has its amateur magazines, but generally they know who is good. Even an amateur magazine wouldn't include anything saying Picasso is no good!

With the joiners I'm trying to bring the picture to you. I'm positive it does make you feel closer because it puts you there, in a sense, at my feet: the world then begins with you. The picture of my mother on the cover of the Japanese catalogue* comes right to where you would be standing, and at least breaks the window idea. There might still be a door, but you do go into the picture.

PJ: At least a door takes you ...

DH: ... to the floor, that's it, and a window does not. George Rowley also said that out of doors our eyes were forced to move about to encompass the scene. Well, that's true indoors, that's true anywhere. In fact, the closer things are to us, the more our eyes have to move. With the joiners the effect is a very strong one of putting you into the place. It gives you a

---

* Catalogue of the show 'David Hockney – New Work with a Camera', Nishimura Gallery, Tokyo, 3–29 October 1983.

much greater feeling of being there. Although it appears that we don't look at the ground, we do if we move, we scan it very carefully and quickly. If there was a great big black hole we would not walk into it. Now, there *are* other ways of doing this, because the Chinese scroll also takes you into the picture. You're not a spectator outside, you seem to have gone in, you are walking down the streets, as it were. That's due to the fact that the focus is moving and so are you. So it's all related in a way, whereas the static nature of the viewing position, whether in a photograph or in a Canaletto, results in a fixed scene from a very fixed point. You don't move. In the Canaletto painting at least your eye can move – it's following the hand making the depiction and therefore the time depicted is there.

You have to learn quite a few things to be able to see another way, and to be able to depict that way of seeing on the canvas. Unless you learn about your own movement and your own body, you still look at things the old way. There are people who try to put the whole room into a painting – there is an English painter whose canvases are often oddly shaped because he's putting in a whole room and the floor. You don't feel the body is moving there (the painting is still actually seen from one point), but just trying to take on more – rather like the way the wide-angle lens sees. Whereas, if you take in a head movement, that point becomes much bigger, and becomes what George Rowley calls 'the moving focus'. Movement is life, essentially, isn't it?

PJ: Do you think the fact that the camera obscura couldn't deal with a depth of focus simply meant that the view was always outwards – horizontal?

DH: You see the camera obscura is, essentially, a window in a wall, and that's what the image is going to represent, it's as simple as that. We realize now that the tripod is like the easel, and the lens of the camera is a hole in a room. That's what camera means in Italian – a room.

PJ: Do you think that there's anything that photography can do that other fine art techniques have not been able to achieve?

DH: Yes, there must be things – one thing photography *can* do is to make replicas of things. With the aid of photography we certainly make very good replicas of drawings – very, very good. You have to be quite an expert to tell the difference. I think there are moments of documentation – when photography achieves something. Cartier-Bresson has made some memorable photographs, if you think of the family picnicking, or the one with the girl at the end of the war – 'The Informer'. I can't remember every detail, but it's a very strong image that goes into your head, such is the power of photography, and there aren't many images like that considering the millions that exist.

We don't know exactly why it works that way. Would the photograph mean the same to anyone? Both those photographs I mentioned mean quite a bit to us because any English person has seen a family like that, or they have picnicked like that themselves. The war pictures – 'The Informer' in particular – are very strong, I think. Cartier-Bresson is the photographer who made the point about the decisive moment. You see that moment instantly and then other forces come into play – other pictures, actually – and that photograph triggers other pictures in our minds. Now, painting may or may not do that. It doesn't have to in order to be enjoyed, necessarily. But photography is not going to go away, so why are there so few of these memorable images, considering that the amount of paintings made is far smaller? I am trying to find the *good* points about photography, through all this criticism!

PJ: I want to follow that idea through about pictures having resonances, or bringing to play other images. Can you expand on that?

DH: With the photograph that resonance is the reason that the image works. With painting it does not necessarily have to happen. There's a difference. Now when that happens it's triggering images in your memory, isn't it? In a sense your memory might be making them. These photographs are powerfully still, aren't they? It's the stillness you remember.

PJ: But think about 'The Informer' photograph. There's a

woman actually striking the informer. Her face is frozen but she's in the middle of a violent action; it can capture that.

DH: It does capture that, and you can understand that the woman who is striking her was wounded in the war, psychologically wounded; it's a moment of revenge, it's overcome her. And that's the moment we see her. But it might be a one-sided picture of her. There might have been a moment or two later when there was a flash of compassion within her. We don't know. She might have continued to be angry but we can't tell from the picture. Well, you could say that the movie would tell us that, but in the presence of a movie camera people don't behave that way, do they? Cartier-Bresson, after all, had a technique that was very unobtrusive. I'm sure she hardly noticed him, hardly noticed his camera, whereas with a movie camera she might well have stopped herself acting in the passion of the moment. I'm trying to question all the

things surrounding the image.

PJ: Photography has falsely extended a particular aspect of her character by freezing it and making it into a classic image.

DH: Surely there must have been moments in her character when she would have had a little compassion. I think we're all weak, but some people see the cruel person simply as a hideous monster: there are people who understand that behind it is a weak human being. We're now talking about a personal view of it all. I know people are monsters; I know they are wicked and cruel, but I also believe that we're all weak as well. But we strive, don't we? We know what is good and we strive towards it.

However, this photograph makes you think of the war — this was 1945 and there had been informers in France who had been callous and cruel and thoughtless, and to gain something for themselves they had given other people away

Dessau: Exposing a Gestapo Informer, 1945
photograph by Henri Cartier-Bresson

and caused a lot of misery. We all have anger and we know that the woman striking the informer could be ourselves. We are all capable of that and we all have these moments of hatred. It doesn't matter about the side of the war, whether we are German or French, it's not political, in that sense, it's about emotion, the emotion of anger. It couldn't be posed – the face wouldn't look like that. I was telling you about the book [by Spender] the other day – it struck me there finally that the expressions on the faces could not have been posed. If I'd posed those pictures identically today it wouldn't look the same because people don't *feel* the same. They don't feel threatened as directly as those people were threatened. Maybe these are the reasons why many people say that Cartier-Bresson is an artist.

But what are those old photographs going to look like in another fifty years? We're going to look back, naturally. There are a few photographs that mean an incredible lot to us, although they might not mean anything to another person. We all have those, the family snaps, however bad they are technically. They all trigger memories, outside any aesthetic ideas.

PJ: With Bresson we're talking about quite a finely-tuned aesthetic, aren't we? And that aesthetic reveals itself in the rules of composition he followed, which are still being adhered to, unless all those are going to be totally smashed, and I doubt that. In fifty years they will still be exceptional pieces of photography.

DH: We don't know that for sure. Take a fourteenth-century woodcut – it looks different to us now than it did to somebody in the fourteenth century, but there are certain things that still work in it. We know that it's a product of the hand – again we go back to this! We used to talk about primitive art – we talk about it a lot less now – but one reason we talked

Untitled sequel to the photograph opposite,
Henri Cartier-Bresson

about it was that certain forms looked very different; we were so used to European forms. We can understand Cortés coming here to Mexico and seeing the art and wondering whether it was devil-worship. Three hundred years later we're so removed from it that we can see the beauty of the form and realize that it is sophisticated, not primitive in any way. But it could be that the photograph is a primitive picture.

We don't know what the world will look like in a hundred years. We look back and we say: we've been looking at photographs for a hundred years. We have indeed, and only our attitude to the subject matter has changed. But that might not go on for ever, because the photograph hasn't changed in a hundred years, the way of seeing (and we're back to that) is precisely the same. But one suspects that it might be a *genuinely* primitive picture, in which case it might well be seen differently. This is all speculation – we won't be there to see it, but we do know that each age looks at the past differently. The past has changed, and I might have strayed from your question, actually!

[After an interval]

DH: The Spaniards came to Mexico and South America and found a civilization that in some ways was incredibly sophisticated and advanced, but in other ways was unbelievably primitive and evil. They saw the sculpture as hideously ugly; it must have looked that way to them. I try to imagine what *we* would feel, but we can't put ourselves in that position. With a leap of the imagination we can try. When the Spaniards looked at this sculpture they associated it with foul practices and with devil worship, so the beauty of its forms was irrelevant to them. The more we hear about a society which killed people all the time for sacrifice, the more difficult it is to understand them. It's beyond the imagination almost! But that culture was smashed, built upon, and naturally some of their ways and beliefs blended into the new religion which the Spaniards brought with them. It blended amazingly well for all kinds of reasons.

It wasn't until the later nineteenth century that people began to take a real interest in that art which was called

Aztec and Mayan artefacts at The Anthropology Museum, Mexico City, photographs by Paul Joyce

'Primitive' Pre-Colombian Art. Well, we've seen several things in the museum in Mexico City and we know they are not primitive, they are highly sophisticated and skilfully made, and the people who made them worked on the same problems that artists work on today. So it has taken three hundred years before we can see that form and divorce it from its original purpose. It is clear that we see a beauty the Spaniards did not see. We're looking at the same objects. They have not changed themselves, but the minds being brought to look at the objects have changed.

We need people now who would agree that in another hundred years the movie of today will look primitive. Even then we cannot say what the movie in a hundred years will look like. We are interested to know what form it will take, what future pictures will evolve, but it's pointless to sit down and try to speculate. It grows slowly. We do know we change. We've observed that from the past. So there's no reason to suppose that it won't go on. It would be naive to assume that we've reached a culmination, that this is it. But the fact that some photographs work in a special way is true. They do. It

would be silly to deny it. When I say that photography is a failure, I'm not denying the resonance of some great photographs. That's obvious – it's in front of your eyes. I'm saying that we don't know how that resonance might alter in time.

PJ: When you were talking about the naive work of art, it occurred to me that maybe, if photography is truly a naive art, it's been adopted and made to look very sophisticated in a much shorter time than it took for true primitive art to be seen as sophisticated. Is there a parallel there?

DH: What do you mean by 'true primitive art'? You have to say what that is. True primitive art is art that's not art, that is incompetent art.

PJ: I'm trying to think of a way to draw a comparison with photography, which seems to be a highly sophisticated art, skill or technique because of the complexity of detail which it achieves...

DH: Well, that in itself doesn't make it sophisticated...

PJ: No. It is actually primitive. I think you're right. But it

seems to be sophisticated. We have been fooled, perhaps, by the surface of it.

DH: Well, that's my basic argument. That's my main thesis, in fact. The leading question is 'What can photography do?' And I did state one clear thing it can do – it can copy itself, certainly it can copy another photograph perfectly. It was no joke when I said that the best photographs were of drawings or paintings. You must deal with that side of photography and say what it can do – and that aspect of it has enriched our visual experience enormously.

PJ: It's given us photographic art books, it's opened up that for us.

DH: Yes, you can have a book of Rembrandt etchings that aren't printed from the plates, and you can buy it quite cheaply. That kind of reproduction is very, very close to the original – the subtleties are not there, but a great deal is there. It's the great photographic skill, and it's a lot less mechanical than we think.

PJ: You've actually taken the mechanics and extended the possibilities. You've done that with smaller formats and so you've already taken it a step beyond the purely mechanical reproduction of a particular object. And with these three-dimensional paintings of yours, you're actually representing things from many points of view. It's the first time I've seen this in a single, albeit composite, image. And that's what I'm trying to get at – the beyond. You've made the point, and very eloquently, about how photography can copy, and now we see you extending that facility.

DH: Well, when it's not a flat surface, the problems occur. In copying the flat surface, the photograph has no illusion to it, of space or depth, it's just like itself – a flat surface.

PJ: You're talking now about the copying of your photographs here in Mexico, or just copying anything?

DH: *Any* reproduction of a painting.

PJ: But how else can the photograph be used, by an artist, say, or even, God help us, the photographer?

DH: Well, the one problem that I have now is that, because of what I've gone into, I begin to see the ordinary photograph slightly differently. And I can't help it now – there's no way I can go back. It's entered my mind; it's the way the mind questions something.

PJ: What are those differences?

DH: The differences are that the photograph becomes more and more excessively frozen. I see it in a way that the ordinary viewer, who does not question it, does not see it. Each of us *sees* the photograph differently.

For instance, there are six portraits here – twelve portraits of ladies' faces – a picture of your mother's face, who I've never seen, and a picture of my mother's face. So however you look at these, one photo stands out, however good or bad it is. The one that's standing out to you does not stand out to me unless it jumps out for aesthetic reasons, formal reasons. So, we are seeing different things, aren't we? Even on this flat surface. We're seeing different things here in this exhibition and we're seeing different things out in the world. And it gets down to this disturbing area – it makes you think that there's no such thing as objective vision at all. Do we actually think there is? We certainly think there are objective judgments and subjective judgments. The scientists think there is objective vision.

PJ: The microscope . . .

DH: Yes, on the other hand, if I look down the microscope and the scientist looks down the microscope we may see the same thing, but there's a different meaning. Does it mean that a scientist trained the same way sees the same thing? It could be only a small portion of what is there. He or she is looking for a particular thing. But if he's not looking for anything special there's the question of aesthetic pleasure.

PJ: That might be true for you but not for him.

DH: Well, it's also there for him, but his mind might block it out by looking for something else. What I'm saying is that there's so much there. But I still believe that there is an objective view, and I'm trying to look at it in every way because it's a disturbing thing, isn't it? Don't people feel that?

PJ: Well, I don't. But then we can look at the things we do agree about. Take that Cartier-Bresson picture of the informer: it's a famous picture, it's in *The Decisive Moment*, it's been reprinted, every history of photography will probably include that image. And you and I are not sitting here talking with it in front of us. Yet I guarantee that we can both remember details from it. And we have seen it in a very similar way. We see a number of things in a similar way.

DH: It's gone into our memories because you're interested in depictions, as I am, and you look at them in a certain way as well. There's a vast number of people who might have seen the picture but who wouldn't remember it in the same way. But why did it go into our memories? Not just from the emotions involved in the depiction. There are other reasons, there must be. We might be going round in circles here!

PJ: But are those reasons actually to do with inherent qualities of medium, which do make it special and able to be used?

DH: I don't know. There's one problem that you have to keep there in front of you when you're photographing. It's right there in front of the camera, it's not a problem that the painter has. I made an example with the Picasso painting: if you had a photograph of an identical subject, some soldiers shooting at women and children, if it was staged, it would be obvious. But if you have a photograph that was not staged, the effect is totally different from a painting because of the fact that the man was *there*. This causes a different effect, a profoundly different effect because it shocks people.

The photograph can shock us more than the painting because people know the photographer was there. The photo of the little girl running down the road in Vietnam is tolerated only because she's some distance away. We know about telephoto lenses, so we understand that the space between the man making the depiction and the girl is considerable. If the distance was not apparent the photograph would horrify us, not just because of the girl who is burning, but because of the photographer who, we know, was not helping. He probably stood there with a light meter and so on. You couldn't make a joiner of that subject – the portrait would be far too strong. That's why there's a certain optimism in all these joiners – there is a love of the world.

There's a debate about pornography and the fact that a great deal of it depicts cruelty and sadism. We're never sure whether it's posed or not, but if it's not, you tend to know because you become that person, the depictor, and you begin to get his feelings. It's easier to pose cruelty than it is to pose two people enjoying something. Faking two people enjoying themselves is much more difficult, and much more difficult to depict. But debates about pornography never get to this idea. Two people's sexual enjoyment has certainly been depicted in painting and drawing because, of course, the third person doesn't have to be there. They could have been one of the actors in the drama. This is not so in photography. If you see two people making love in a photograph you know there must be three people there. Well, to a great number of people this fact makes the occasion unprivate and they do not feel they can express themselves. The kind of people who like it would probably be exhibitionists. And for someone who has looked at what most people would consider to be lots and lots of pornographic or erotic pictures, I think the kind of joy we're talking about is very, very rarely depicted.

It could be that the sexual act is the ultimate creative act. There are many ways of looking at it, but it could well be that it presents a problem for photography similar to the problem of genuine documentary cruelty. The way a painter can see or feel something is very different. Take Picasso's major painting in 1951, for instance – he had never been to Korea, and I don't think he was making it as Communist propaganda, but he was simply moved by what he saw as yet another war. He'd seen one in Europe as an artist resident in Paris, and he saw, as everybody must have seen, photographs of the results of that war, of people at the fronts, and the incredible cruelty and madness. It must have affected everybody. I can remember seeing photographs of people like skeletons. Clearly, Picasso felt very deeply about it and he made a picture that is illustrative, but I think he was dealing as well with the problem the camera has because of its nature.

Trang Bang, South Vietnam, June 8th 1972,
photograph by Nguyen Kong (Nick Ut)

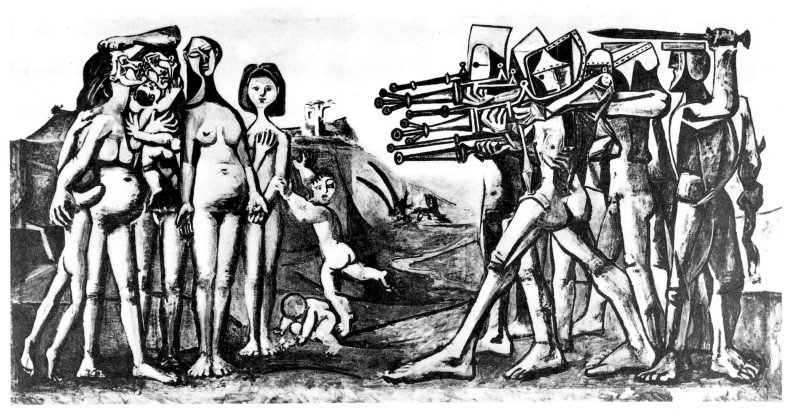

Massacre in Korea, 1951 by Pablo Picasso

Even if the camera is a medium, it has a quality unlike all other artistic mediums. In a sense it's autobiographical because it's about you, it's something in front of you. Painting might be autobiographical but not necessarily in its subject matter. Part of the subject matter of a photograph is that the photographer is there, and it's an aspect that makes it peculiar. I accepted this and I'm dealing with it in order to emphasize it. Although it's a perfectly simple truth, at times it's forgotten. It's not forgotten in cases like the little girl burning in Vietnam, when what we're witnessing horrifies us because we do immediately think of the person there seeing it.

PJ: Photography can question the relationship of the photographer to the event quite powerfully. For example, in the famous bayoneting in the polo field in India, photographers were actually called to the event to give it publicity, and they all walked away except one or two.* They stayed and shot the photographs within a few feet of people being bayoneted to death and there was a great debate about whether they should have stayed or left. The debate is what you're talking about, isn't it?

DH: Well, it's a moral question, but it is peculiar to photography, that's what I'm pointing out. With a photograph we can't question the fact that someone *was* bayoneted to death. There have been pretty gory movies but we don't believe them, actually. I met a guy who made these 'snuff' movies, and I'd never heard the term so I asked what it was and he said: somebody gets killed. Somebody might *apparently* get

---

* Horst Faas and Michel Laurent of Associated Press – who won the Pulitzer Prize for their efforts.

killed on television every night, but in 'snuff' movies it is real. Well, how do you know? There are all kinds of ways of faking it. You can fake it in a movie pretty convincingly.

I said that you couldn't make a joiner of the little girl burning in Vietnam. You *can*, but it would display an unbelievably cold view of humanity. The fact that the little girl is running, she's blurred – all this tells you the photographer saw it. If she had run towards him he might have put his camera down, put out the flames – we assume that he would have done what a decent human being would do. We assume that the photographer is a decent human being.

I've read that Hitler made movies out of people being strangled and so on. Apparently the films were even made with the intention of showing the public, until they realized it was so revolting. It's far more revolting that the depictor could be so cold. We know there are executioners and we might not like them, we know it goes on, but the depiction of it is something else. I think if this happens we descend into a terrible side of ourselves when we wish, on the whole, to raise ourselves up. What we're talking about is a moral issue, but it is peculiar to the nature of photography.

PJ: Are you saying then that by being there you're going to a point which is beyond imaginative possibility?

DH: I said that we would be horrified, but there are some people who would not be. I would have to say that they are evil, that this is the depiction of evil. Yet, we know that evil exists and that it's powerful, but the fact of depicting it seems to double it. It's very different when the painter depicts it – Picasso in his painting is depicting evil, but he's clearly stating that it *is* evil. It's very, very clear that he's on the side of humanity which we assume, or I assume, we all are, or should be. It's a question that links up with this other one – is it easier to depict cruelty or joy? Certainly, descriptions of hell have been much more vivid than descriptions of heaven. It's harder to conceive what heaven is. Does that mean that we are closer to hell, that there's so much evil in us that our imaginations can get to that more easily? In fact, most depictions of heaven seem to be a bit boring!
[After an interval]

DH: The camera seems to be an instrument that's always confirming perspective, so you have to go back and deal with that. The painter has to deal with that. You can't go on ignoring it. Picasso made marvellous discoveries, but he just ignored the camera. He knew somebody else would deal with it. That's why it had to be done. It's only part of a journey, it's not an end in itself to me. You make some beautiful pictures along the way, but it's leading to something else. It's leading to more vivid depictions.

PJ: But when you got that far with the Mulholland Drive painting, you went back to the camera in order to get to your next stage.

DH: Then I realized that I had to do something with the camera after that. I knew you had to move the camera, but I didn't know how. I groped my way on, and I went back to painting. And then I did the Stravinsky in between so it waited a year. But all the time it was in my head, so maybe it was better that way.

PJ: In moving back to the camera, if you hadn't actually exploded the frame you would have had an insoluble problem. You had to do something drastic.

DH: These ideas may have started slowly but once I got into it, there was a time when I just could not stop. The photography was like that. I could not stop even though gluing the pictures down at times got boring. You couldn't just give them to somebody else to glue because that's a very deep part of it. When you are gluing them you learn how to see each frame, relating one to another, and that's not easy. I am positive that you must never cut any of the photographs because it destroys the time sequence. It stops it.

PJ: You have to overlap them.

DH: You must not cut them. If you did, you would be trying to get an illusion another way. You might get an interesting picture of another kind, but it won't lead you forwards because you would have destroyed part of what it's about. Cutting pictures up destroys the flow of time. You must ask why you would want to cut it? You'd want to cut it because

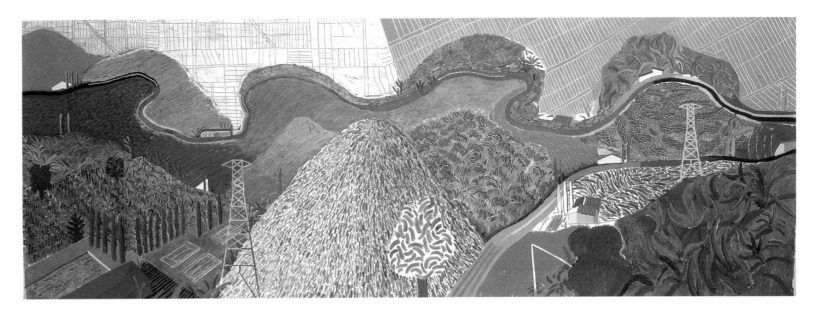

Mulholland Drive: The Road to the Studio,
1980 (painting)

you hadn't seen it properly in the right time. I told you that my brother did some cutting and something happened, it seemed to become more like a montage, instead of a collage. I think you sense then a halt in time. The reason you want to cut the photos is to create an illusion that's based on a single picture, an ordinary picture. Consequently, what I was concerned with would have been destroyed. I decided very early on *not* to cut the pictures up. Wouldn't we then be doing what the Victorian photographers did by making a picture out of eight negatives? It's the same thing, really, as cutting up pictures, like Bill Brandt putting the sky in from another picture. I decided not to do that for another reason – it's harder, but I think you keep the flow of time.

PJ: Do you think that when we look at them, as an audience, aware of what the picture is giving us, that the underneath part of the picture we don't see is still something we're aware of?

DH: Yes, I think it relates to the thing on top. It's often the same thing from a slightly different viewpoint.

PJ: So our imagination comes into play as to what may be underneath and how it relates to the image you have overlaid. Do you think people will know instinctively that there is a physical overlap of images?

DH: Yes, and they know that what's underneath must be similar. It's not covering up something completely different.

PJ: Well, in that case you're talking about something that isn't a flat surface because it must, by definition, have depth to it even though you can't see the depth.

DH: It has a depth, yes. Real photographs are always better than reproductions, aren't they? Partly through scale, but partly through their physicality. And I realized another wonderfully mad paradox. These works of mine are photographs that can't essentially be reproduced, which is not true of any other photograph. You can make a photograph of another photograph and hardly know the difference, but in this case it would never be the same.

PJ: That's very interesting, because the Polaroids actually as objects have depth to them, and your joiners have depth because they overlap, so you have succeeded in building depth into an apparently flat surface. Isn't that why they can't be reproduced? You can't reproduce that depth.

DH: The real ones are much more effective, partly to do with scale, but partly to do with the fact that to reproduce them incredibly well you'd need a very, very big camera. My negative, even if it's on 110 film, is quite big eventually if you

93

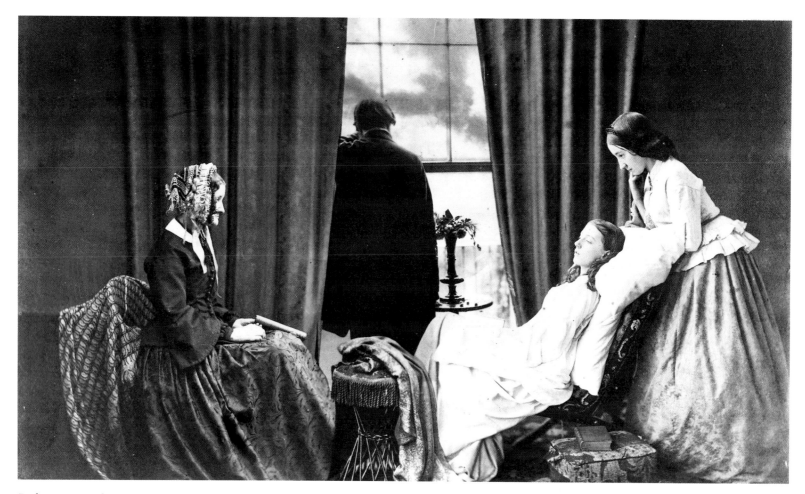

Fading Away (first impression) by Henry Peach Robinson,
composite albumen print from five negatives, 1858

piece it together, isn't it? So it doesn't matter what size the film is, that's another thing. It doesn't matter about exposures. A camera with an automatic exposure is absolutely fine and you learn how to compose to avoid problems.

PJ: It seems to me that when you reject the possibility of cutting up photographs you are adopting a purist stance.

DH: To me cutting only leads to *un*clarity. What did you cut out? Why did you cut it out? Something you didn't like was there, you wanted a sharp edge. There are ways to do it without cutting which would keep the flow of time, keep it moving around and, therefore, the eye moving around. If you cut it the eye will stop or at least have to pause.

PJ: Even if the edge isn't seen. It knows that there's something...

DH: Oh, yes. Because the rectangle's been broken and suddenly the picture is a completely different shape. And people said to me: why don't you trim the white off the Polaroids? Well, one reason was that it would damage them, they would fall apart. But I think the reason they wanted it trimmed off was to make it like – for want of a better expression – an ordinary picture. They think the picture should look like that. The instinct to put the picture in a rectangle is very strong, and with the Polaroids, anyway, you're always making rectangles. When I was doing the small Polaroids of the *Rossignol* piece James [the photographer] was disturbed because the bottom line wasn't going to be straight. But I pointed out that it was inevitable and you had to accept it – in fact, if you did it that way there was something quite honest about it. It seemed better to me than cutting the photographs.

94

PJ: Do you see any fundamental difference in concept between the Polaroid joiners and the later 35mm and 120 photocollages?

DH: Oh, yes. The difference is in the way they are constructed. The Polaroid joiner is constructed as you go along. If you can see half the picture, then you've done half the picture. It's done visually, it's more like a drawing. Whereas the other joiner – there are two things – the way you take the pictures, and then the way you join them together. In one sense, joining them together is harder because you find a large number of choices there. They don't actually join together, or one part may join together but another won't, and so on. Some of the choices take quite a while to make. It's like a chess game; you move ahead a little bit and you plan it. I think the two joiners are profoundly different. The Polaroids are done in one go and the others are done in two goes.

PJ: But it seems to me that the Polaroids are not done in one go, but in twenty or two hundred goes, because every time you fit them together you make a choice which affects the taking of the next Polaroid image.

DH: Yes, that may be true, but it's all done at one period. Once you start the Polaroid you have to finish it. I don't think you can go back the day after, whereas, once you start taking the others, the gluing together takes far more than a day, far more. You lay it out, then wait, then think about it. Some I had to lay out twice because the first time it got confused, or if I re-did it, overlapping one picture another way would move it in a different direction – all these are choices that are important.

PJ: Can you tell me something about the physical piecing together of the non-Polaroid joiners? Is there anything akin to painting when you're making those choices and fitting those images together?

DH: Well, it's not the same. In painting the hand is *literally* making the art...

[After an interval]

DH: The joiners are about *you* moving – that's what the principle is, and cubism entails a similar principle. I'm convinced now about cubism – it is not about abstraction at all, it's about the depiction of reality in a more vivid way. We've had the crisis in abstraction and people are now going back to realist painting. They are forced to go back. Cubism can take you on another journey entirely – whereas abstraction only takes you back to the old way of seeing with perspective – that's where it came from, not from cubism. I'm grasping the principle. And it's working in that hotel picture.

PJ: A viewer coming to this for the first time would see, obviously, that the perspective is quite unusual, but they might not say it was a cubist work.

DH: No. They wouldn't associate it with cubism. I know it's from cubism because I can trace where the ideas came from. However, the viewer knows something different is happening. It does work. You *know* those columns are round. There's only one line that tells you, but it does tell you. Each column is seen from a different angle yet it has a unity. The plane of the floor is felt too, isn't it? There are only ten lines but they change direction, each line works. It's very simple, but it does work.

PJ: Tell me about the roof structure, because that gives the most extraordinary effect.

DH: Well, it's going against the laws of perspective as we know them. Those laws have to be based on one point. Each time your eye moves the perspective is actually changing you. This is going to be much more interesting than the camera, because it's about *you* seeing things instead of the one point of the camera seeing things.

PJ: What about the relationship of the floor to the ceiling? Even if you are constructing a different set of perspective rules, do both floor and ceiling have to accord with the same principle or could each follow a different set of rules?

DH: I don't know. After all, the drawing was done instinctively but following a principle. Instinct told me how to do it.

A Walk around the Hotel Acatlan, Mexico, 1985
(painting on two canvases)

Exactly how it's changing I'm not sure, but it is, and the perspective is strange, isn't it?

PJ: Certainly.

DH: Yet it works. You understand it, don't you?

PJ: Oh yes. Absolutely. There is no way that any optical device could represent that. The only way you could do it is by actually splitting the image. Something happens here which is not true to one's remembrance of the object.

DH: But it is true to one's *moving*, that's the point. And I think the photograph has had an incredible influence on us without our knowing it. It's made us see in a strait-jacketed way. And it's mad that we find it difficult to see any other way, but the moment it's demonstrated we see it's true.

PJ: And so what you're saying, actually, is that abstraction and photography have gone in a circle, always returning one to the other. And there's no way to break through that circle. It occurs to me that photography might actually have made people look from a fixed position. Ordinary people, every-body, now stands like a tripod.

DH: Yes, our eyes have been made to do that because we keep seeing photographs and thinking they are true. If we look at life we then discover that the images have affected the way we look. I think that's now obvious, and it puts drawing and painting back into a far more serious position than even I ever thought possible. Only there can we expand our apprehension of things. Although the camera led me into this, it was only in order to break up what was wrong. I knew there was something wrong. And there is still something wrong, even now, and that is the lack of the hand and eye co-ordinating. But what is happening is amazing – you won't have seen a drawing quite like that.

PJ: No, the hotel room is quite different, it takes a moment to realize it, and then, when you do, it's a very exciting journey. The glory is that although it has the economy of Matisse, it has a new consciousness about the way objects appear.

DH: Well, the printers knew there was something going on that was different. They asked me what it was. Why *do* you feel more space here? It's the principle of the moving focus. There's a difference between scientific representation and artistic presentation, and that difference is the hand. The hand and the eye and the heart coming together. It's clear, now, to me. It opens up a new way of seeing which will make us realize that the world does look quite different. And in that sense it's a bit mind-blowing, isn't it?

PJ: Well, my mind is already all over Mexico, but yes!

Los Angeles: June 1984

Back in LA we continued to talk for a few more days. I had started to shoot some of my own 'mosaic' photographic experiments, mainly of David and his travelling companion Gregory Evans in Mexico, and continued with these back in California. The locations for our talks varied between his house and studio off Mulholland Drive, his other studio on Santa Monica Boulevard, and various lunch and dining places. (David has a very good instinct about where to eat, and combines a fine aesthetic judgment on food with a realistic Bradfordian notion of which establishments offer real value for money.)

David rarely draws or photographs formal portraits of strangers or even acquaintances, preferring to concentrate on intimate friends whose features he has come to know over a period of years. One evening, in the middle of our talking, he said, 'I'll photograph you tomorrow.' I duly presented myself next morning, and the day wore on in conversation without any further mention of the photographic session. At about 10 p.m. he suddenly said, 'Come over to the studio', so off we went, put on the lights, and I was ordered into a low-slung chair. He pulled out a large sheet of hand-made paper and began drawing. It was a very peculiar experience, for now David turned his eyes fully on me, and I felt my whole physiognomy under scrutiny – not just the surface but deeper – as one might be sized-up by a surgeon or bone-setter. I could not help but respond with the same kind of intensity. Afterwards he showed me what he'd done, and I saw he'd represented my eyes as deep black holes – a very accurate representation of the kind of penetration I felt sitting in front of him in that chair.

PJ: Isn't it time to say that once one begins to see the world without the restrictions of conventional one-point perspective, everything changes.

DH: It is a vast change. It affects everything, far more than just art. The movie, for instance, is still involved with the old perspective. And although it has advantages and the movie works, nevertheless that too can be made even richer. The wider perspective opens up completely new possibilities of

Paul, Hollywood, March 28th 1987 (crayon and ink)

visual narrative. And when you think about it, I'm right about the narrative aspect. When the figure is static, it's solid, it appears so. If you're still, all the subtleties I'm talking about, the small movements do appear very, very solid. But with the new way of seeing, the volume, the air your body is replacing, is constantly moving and changing. So that opens up the possibilities of narrative, whereas traditional perspective limits it. Even with Caravaggio the narrative is stuck, isn't it?

PJ: Yes, it is. And it is, in a sense, very photographic.

DH: Yes. In Titian's 'Bacchus and Ariadne' – the cloak is frozen in the sky, isn't it?

PJ: Yes, the cloak is for ever stuck there. It's only an extraordinary skill that gives you the impression of movement. In fact, in the Caravaggio, you get a feeling that there is no

movement, you feel that the arm is actually held there.

DH: You have a feeling of depth, but the depth stops movement. It's as if he had to fix the depth. It's amazing, isn't it?

PJ: Very important. It brings you back to people and life and relationships, even if it's just the relation of people to objects.

DH: With these pictures we can really deal with space. The Renaissance wanted to deal with space but they just put it in a strait-jacket. Cubism got out of that and opened up narrative. Unfortunately it looked as if it was leading to abstraction, but abstraction is about the fixing of space and the fixing of shape. Abstraction looks quite different. And the absurdity of attempting narrative in the other way got more and more obvious because the picture was fixed.

PJ: You did say you had to *purge* yourself of photography. That's a very strong word.

DH: Yes, it is. Until it dawns on you that the photograph is the extension of the Renaissance idea, you can't deal with the problems. And *I've* only become convinced of it in the last three months. When I was talking to Melvyn Barge, I didn't say anything about it because it hadn't then dawned on me. But the more you think about it, the more you realize that the photograph has stopped us. It appeared to be the most vivid, authentic representation of what we saw, but it is not.

PJ: That's why the joiners, not the Polaroid joiners, but the other joiners, are so complicated to put together because you're trying to follow a line, not a conventional line of perspective, but a line in your head about the object.

DH: And it's about *you* a lot more than you think.

PJ: So there's always a tension between the image and what you want the image to do, and that's why those joiners are so complex.

DH: Yes, and that's why the instinct is to do with perspective. The moment I started on those early joiners and realized they weren't working out, it became clear that there was another way that didn't depend on rectangles. Then it began to dawn on me that I was breaking something else down. The rectangle was the window, essentially, that we believed in. I was still believing in it to a certain extent. It's hard to break away from it, very, very hard. Why is it so fixed in us? Perspective is only a theoretical abstraction. It is not true to life, no matter what we say. Perspective depends on a fixed point, but if you try to walk up to that point you'd never get there, it's like the end of the rainbow!

PJ: And the joiners, of course, smash the rectangle, because, in laying one across the other, you've already destroyed the rectangle.

DH: Yes, but it took a long time to really smash it because of that instinct. Look at those Grand Canyons I did, I thought that the horizon was horizontal but, look, it's becoming a curve. The curve is about *you*, not the horizon. It's related back to your body.

PJ: And to the movement of a body.

DH: Yes, because your body moving means you're alive. It's telling you you're alive. That's why people react to it. They *feel* more alive. That's why, in the exhibition, people stand in front of them for quite a while. You can't just glance at them and walk back. You can't do that. We like being alive. We choose it. We cling to it.

PJ: But in photography pessimism is easy, that's the other thing, isn't it? I think that photography has actually extended us into an area of cruelty and depression and negativity. When you think of the photographic images that actually stick in the mind, it's the gun going against the Vietnamese, it's the woman falling from the balcony, it's the bayoneting of the troops, it's the Bresson photograph of the informer that we were talking about. I've always thought that photography was about death because it fixes the image. There is nothing life-enhancing about it, finally.

DH: The Bresson photograph about the picnic *is* joyful because we look at it and we're amused – they are rather a fat family, it's about the pleasures of food, and they've probably eaten too much. It's all there. We are amused, and that photograph has a lot of joy, but it's rare.

PJ: But it was not that image we began to talk about. When we sat down to talk about Bresson, we talked about the informer.

DH: That's because it *seems* more fascinating to us. Just as in the novel or anything else, a story about somebody who was very good all their life isn't that interesting. On the other hand, we do, whether we are religious or not, admire saintly people. I would be hard put to criticize Mother Teresa. We think she's a fine and noble human being, don't we, whether we're religious or not? And the point about saints is not that they are absolutely perfect, but that they've struggled to attain something.

I was always fascinated by St Francis of Assisi and his

self-inflicted poverty. He was honest enough to admit that there were moments of ecstasy in it, although it looked as though he was making it terrible for himself. Well, that's what we all want – moments of ecstasy. We're not as foolish there as we are about happiness. We think happiness is not necessarily on an ecstatic level, and so we want it all the time. We can only appreciate ecstasy in these moments, and I think that is also true of happiness. There are glimpses of it, and they should be treasured. People have always said my pictures have a certain happiness about them, and they think that quality lacks seriousness, that it's not true to life. But it *is* true to life in the sense that those glimpses we keep hold of we linger over. We all want them. It doesn't mean to say that the artist who makes them is always happy. He's not. If you want to know the truth, I know what's going on inside me and a great deal of the time I'm not happy. Van Gogh painted generally happy pictures. The great pictures of his last three years look mostly very happy, so he must have had glimpses of happiness. But he knew about unhappiness, he *certainly* knew the opposite. The enemy is blandness, when it's all the same. Twenty-four hours of ecstasy would be bland. There must be a contrast, and art is about contrast, that's how it works.

The snake in the Anthropology Museum in Mexico City, carved out of stone, can be still in one way and the representation of a movable thing in another. We enjoy it almost more than a real snake. That's why art can be magic. The real snake coiling around might run away. But the artist, realizing in it a thing of beauty, makes a representation of it in stone. And it is the contrast between what the stone is, solid and static, and the representation of the snake in another way that gives it its beauty. The plain stone is transformed into a beauty that is art. And whatever it was that made the artist do it, the contrast in the forms makes it interesting, makes it art. Form and content unite here. In abstraction, form is emphasized although the content might have disappeared. In banal illustration the emphasis is all on content with no form, and, frankly, they are both a bit of a bore. The truth is that content and form merge and become one rarely, and when it happens it's magical art. And I think nineteenth-century painting, with

its fixed views, put an emphasis on content, but limited its ability to move through time. The cubists slowly began to put time back. It appeared at first as if it was totally about the plastic, and it is, in a way, but very few people relate cubism to narrative, even now.

PJ: I think we now have to approach the reality, given the lessons that you have taught us, of how you can break through that conventional frame. Then you have to find your own solution. You've found yours photographically and you are translating it back to painting.

DH: In the painting it's working. You don't know where the edge is even. I did a self-portrait – it's made up of a few canvases, but in essence there's no edge to the picture because the mind jumps about, and in jumping about it doesn't need an edge. With the Chinese scroll two edges are gone – the bottom edge and the top edge are there, but the top could be the sky which is infinity, which we understand but cannot grasp. I'm amazed that the art people won't realize what is actually opening up!

PJ: But they won't take photography seriously. Even when *you* practise it, it's going to take a year or two.

They say that photography is truthful, but I think it inclines more to the meretricious. Just keep snapping and you're bound to get a moment of 'reality'!

DH: I've seen professional photographers shoot hundreds of pictures, but they are all basically the same. They are hoping that in one fraction of a second something will make that face look as if there were a longer moment. The fashion photographer normally shoots off rolls of film with the same pose, rolls of it. Then he scrutinizes it, but he's then scrutinizing the image, not the person. It's a kind of backward action. And the laws of chance come into play here, don't they? If you take a hundred, surely one will be good. It could be anybody doing it. One picture must catch something. It's the old polyphoto idea. Well, painting or drawing doesn't work that way at all. It can't. But I think the best portrait photography is made by a photographer who feels a strong sense of empathy with the subject. In that case probably a scrutiny has been made over a

Sunday on the Banks of the Marne
photograph by Henri Cartier-Bresson, 1938

period of time before the picture was taken. Usually portrait photography is just a cosmetic image – that's all it is. I remember David Bailey did a photo of me in the sixties, and he told me to stand like a bat, or something. It tells you very little about me.

PJ: Like a bat?

DH: Well, he said: hold your sleeves out, like that; but I did it and that's all there was.

PJ: It's not far from Annie Leibovitz posing you with the red pullover in the desert, is it?

DH: It's very similar. I don't think it could possibly tell you very much about the person. The difference between what you might call a very great photographer and a very good photographer is not as much as the difference between a very great painter and a very good painter. I can think of the difference between Rembrandt and one of his contemporaries who you would call very good. The difference is still very great, whereas the difference between – well, how many great photographers are there? Just name one and the difference between him and any other good photographer is much slighter.

PJ: To the point that the photograph taken by the lesser photographer could be mistaken . . .

DH: Whereas no student of Rembrandt's could be mistaken, not really. You don't have to be too much of an expert to know. Also the laws of chance might work so that an amateur might take a very, very good picture, but he's no chance of *painting* like that.

PJ: But there simply aren't great amateur artists, are there? Look at Winston Churchill's work! Your work as an artist,

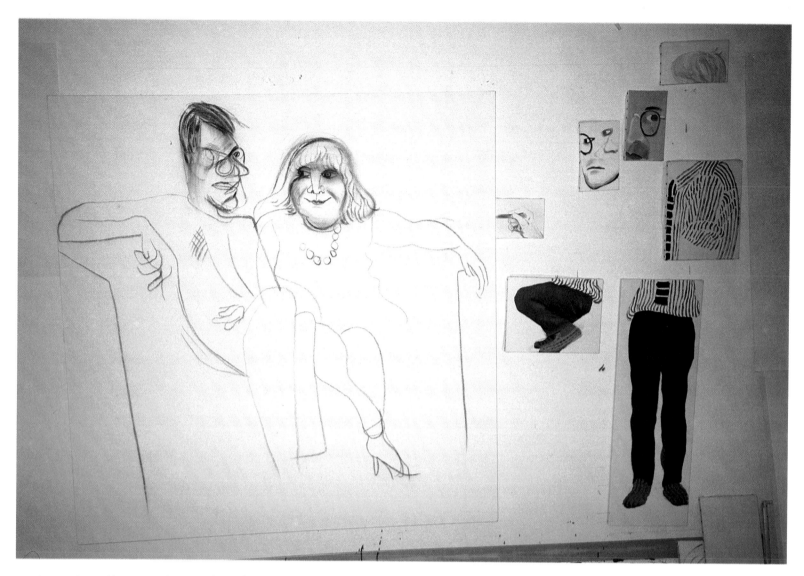

In the Studio, self-portrait by David Hockney alongside an
unfinished portrait by him of David and Ann Graves,
photograph by Paul Joyce, 1985

and as a photographer, brings people back emotionally to
their own bodies. The modern world has taken the emotions
out.

DH: It was the photograph that took away the body. The
photographer has no evidence of the hand to make his eye
move about to give him life. So it seems as if his body isn't
there.

PJ: And this is why photographs seem cold.

DH: If the eye moves, you feel your body move. That's what
it's about. This is the bottom line in the end. We're not there,
but we're getting close to it. We've gone across the threshold,
haven't we? A threshold that now convinces us of the damage
the photograph has done. That's what I think.

PJ: It's taken us away from ourselves. That's why it's so
much a product of the twentieth century. Modern man is
actually disconnected from his own emotions.

DH: And the depictions most often seen are disconnecting him more. Or they might be the reason he'd disconnected from them anyway.

PJ: So the circle is a vicious one. It was certainly damaging me.

DH: It was doing damage to me: it was holding me down. I *had* to go into it. I do like to talk about it because talking sorts it out for me. The moment I talk, things become a bit clearer.

PJ: But you're talking all the time to yourself, aren't you?

DH: Yes, but I don't talk *loudly* to myself. When I'm talking to someone else I'm saying something and hearing it. It might sound a bit mad but ...

PJ: No, the madness is the other way, when there is no outlet and it remains in your head. As soon as you get it out and hear it back, either it makes sense or it's nonsense.

DH: The first lecture I gave on photography was in Auckland. Nobody left, but I was groping around because I don't write lectures down. I then gave the lecture later in London, and it was much more coherent because I'd given it once. I had heard it before! There's a wonderful line from Stan Laurel in a Laurel and Hardy movie: he's reading a letter to Oliver saying he's been left a lot of money and Oliver says: that's fantastic! And Stanley says: well, what's fantastic? Oliver replies: you just read it! And Stanley says: yes, but I wasn't listening. I loved it! It sounds like nonsense, but it isn't.

PJ: It all made sense this morning.

DH: Maybe it was that half-bottle of Taittinger!

New York:
November 1984

In November 1984 David invited me over to New York for an opening of new work at the André Emmerich Gallery. This consisted of large oils, paintings, drawings and photographic pieces. It was the first public exposure of the extraordinary life-sized photographic study of Theresa Russell as Marilyn Monroe in Insignificance. *Her husband (and director of the film) Nicolas Roeg had commissioned this directly from David for use in the picture, and David told me it took him four attempts (with his tiny Pentax) to get it to his own satisfaction. He used up his fee in film stock and processing alone. It is one of the very few nude female studies that David has done, and became an exercise for him to achieve a graphically acceptable image of a figure showing front and back at the same time. (He later showed me examples of Picasso's preoccupation with the same artistic, as opposed to visual, problem.) This picture attracted more attention than any other single piece in the show.*

In New York we talked at the Mayflower Hotel, in David's room and in the coffee shop, walking along Central Park South, and in a couple of restaurants at the top end of Broadway.

DH: The issue of the objective viewpoint is being raised constantly, I think, in other forms. People don't realize that it *is* the same issue. Here's an example – the recent case in America of CBS being sued by General Westmoreland.* CBS were saying that theirs was a neutral viewpoint – that was their defence. The whole case fizzled out because ultimately you can't defend a neutral viewpoint. It's always the same problem really – there is no neutral observer. That's what you come to. Well, perspective, one-point perspective, is all based on an idea of the neutral observer – that you, the viewer, are not there, but there is a viewer outside of us. And that, ultimately, is the photographic flaw. It's the perspective

flaw magnified because of the time problem in the photograph. Have you ever read anything in a photographic or art magazine about the problems of perspective?

PJ: Never.

DH: Well, for three hundred years there were debates about it. Artists knew there was something seriously wrong with it; good artists certainly did. If you look at a Velázquez, there are actually a few viewpoints put in. Now, this is not possible in a photograph unless you begin to do something like I'm doing, unless you begin to make a collage. Then you are putting more perspectives there. Well, I think the Panofsky essay† is the best on this subject. It's being translated now, but it's never been translated into English before and it was written in 1926! In the essay he even mentions quantum flow, which perspective cannot deal with. Now, the idea that perspective is about our attitude to space and us in it is clearly taken from what the Italians were doing. People have forgotten that Brunelleschi and della Francesca set out deliberately to make a new space. Now, we should do that too.

One senses an incredible need to make a new definition, a new attitude, which the camera cannot deal with, nor can the computer if it just works from a camera angle. All it can do is

---

* In January 1982 CBS ran a documentary, *The Uncounted Enemy: A Vietnam Deception*, in which General William Westmoreland was alleged to have been at the centre of a 'conspiracy at the highest levels of military intelligence' to mislead the American President and the public about the success of a war of attrition against Vietnamese insurgents. Four months later unorthodox procedures used in making the programme were uncovered and CBS ordered an investigation but announced that it 'stood by the broadcast'. A five-month libel trial ensued but Westmoreland withdrew his case before a verdict could be reached, while claiming that he had achieved the affirmation of his honour that he had sought.
† 'Die Perspektiv als "symbolische Form"' (Hamburg, 1927).

Nude, 16th June 1984
(photographic collage)

turn it round, but it can't actually alter its shape, which I found I could do in the joiners like the desk picture.* In my lecture I talked about the reverse perspective of the desk and what it means. If only I'd photographed the desk at the same time in a traditional way so you could see both, then it would be very clear what the difference is. Mind you, I did it in the Ryoanji Garden pictures, and one is a triangle because it's seen from one point and the other is a rectangle because you move. And the rectangle is true, which means that our memory of it must be a memory of movement. It all keeps coming back to movement and non-movement.

PJ: If you think about the camera obscura, and the fact that

once you had a fixed perspective and a lens the world seemed to be ordered, it must have seemed they made order out of chaos, and that's why we keep returning to that notion. We don't like chaos: we prefer order.

DH: Yes, that's it, but the perspective that gave order to them will not give order to us. We have to make another order. The idea that perspective is, in Gombrich's unfortunate phrase, 'a conquered reality', is like the ideas of the physicists of those times who thought they had conquered reality. That was the phrase in use in the late nineteenth century. They've learned the lesson – there's far more to discover than we think. We have not conquered reality at all. The idea that the photograph is representing it has to be attacked. I'm deeply convinced about that. Of course, photographers, intelligent

---

* 'The Desk, July 1st, 1984' (see page 128).

The Flagellation of Christ by Piero della Francesca

people, seem to have misunderstood it. Ordinary photographers just don't know what they are talking about.

PJ: They don't want to listen. Where would that leave them?

DH: Yes . . . and I think then the whole thing begins to open up. You realize it affects politics, it affects everything, because it totally affects our way of seeing the world, and feeling it, doesn't it?

PJ: Yes, and what interests me particularly about your letter to R. B. Kitaj is that you say quantum physics has had something to do with the bomb, but your investigations of quantum physics made you see that the danger we face is to do with the way we perceive the world.

DH: This is what I'm beginning to believe: the power that was released by those physical discoveries in the form of a bomb is also there to be released by us in other forms if we look at it in the right way. We've got the bomb: it will not go away, no matter what disarmament conferences say. Deep in our hearts is the knowledge of how to make it. And it can always be made, even if every one was destroyed and we signed papers and everything, we can always make one again quite quickly. Any large war would in future involve it. It's naive to think that it wouldn't. We must begin to look at the world in another way. And the minute you do it becomes more intimate. Look at my photograph of the desk – it's more intimate, we are more in it. Well, of course, the more I read, the more these ideas are confirmed. My instinct has been telling me that and the scientific reading is also saying that.

I found it fascinating that we still look at the world in the same way. We wonder what it would be like to go to the other side of the universe in a spaceship, but we'll realize one day that of course we're already there. There is another way. Once you're aware of it, you're actually there. The mechanics of actually moving through that space would be impossible because of the enormous size. And so it's that other way that eventually we'll discover. In the old perspective you are totally rigid. The furthest point from you is theoretically infinity, which means if the infinite is God, it's always a long way away. You never get there. One hundred per cent of our images in the world are like that. When you reverse the perspective, that point is movement, you're moving. Infinity then is everywhere, including in you, which is far more interesting theologically, isn't it? God is then within us, and actually we are part of God. Ultimately it leads you to an idea of wholeness.

When you put it that way to people, they say: that's all right but how can you alter things? You then realize perspective must be altered, so how come photography goes merrily off on its own? That's why Waldemar Pipsqueak from the *Guardian*, talking about some Italian painters on television, said 'They came from Florence – the city of perspective.' It never occurred to him that the very image you are seeing of *him* is totally one-point perspective with a history that dates back to Florence. He thinks perspective is a kind of neutral thing, that it is just what's there. That attitude will cause unbelievable confusion. So he separates art from that picture of him, as if it had nothing to do with it.

But art was always concerned with making things more vividly real to experience. When they saw Giotto's work, they didn't say: God, this is a new, difficult art to grasp; they said: oh, it's more vivid and more real, and therefore we're moved. And they were. That is the story. And it's true also of Picasso. At first that was difficult to grasp because the jump was very great from the perspective picture. And we would have understood the problem much more readily but photography came in the way. Photography is only a mechanical picture of our attitude to space since the Renaissance. That's all it is. Therefore, if we wish to change that attitude and become aware, the photograph must be deeply involved. But photography critics have not been critical enough. They have always accepted it as if it were fixed. But the issue is going to get gigantic. Artists must be involved in it. It's too vast for them to ignore now. The evidence is strong, the manifestations are constantly around now, even in other forms – the idea of measurement.

I pointed out that Bill Rubin* refers to distortion in primitive sculpture in a sense that even he hasn't grasped. He thinks

---

* William S. Rubin, writer on art, and author of *Pablo Picasso: A Retrospective*.

A Visit with Christopher and Don, Santa Monica Canyon 1984
(painting on two canvases)

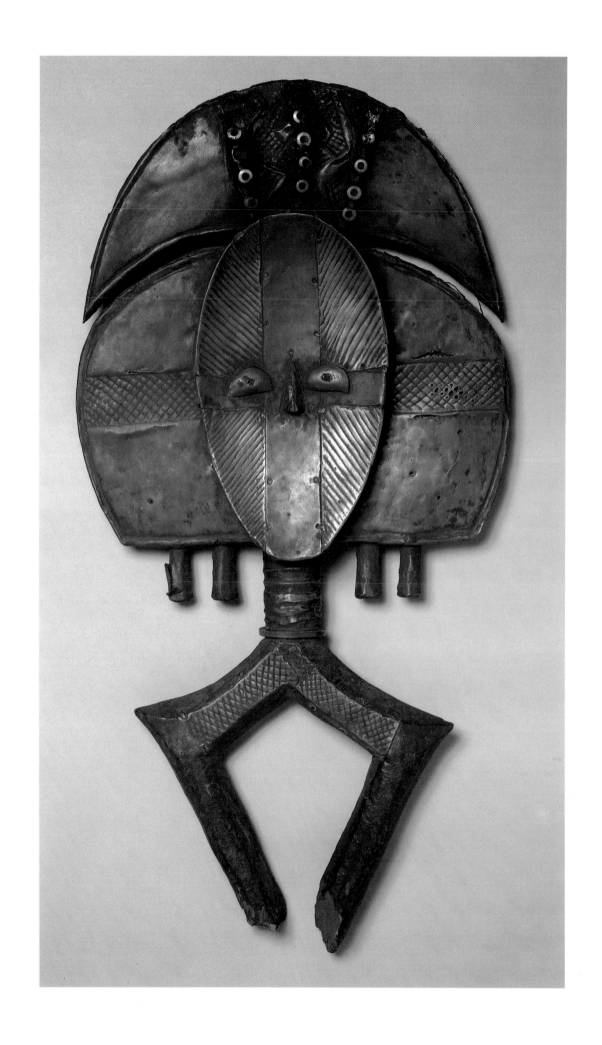

they based their idea on the fact that art is not for everybody. If the primitive making his African sculpture had taken that line, he would have held up his sculpture and everybody would have been baffled. What is it? What is it about? It wouldn't have worked, would it? He wanted it to frighten them or please them, or whatever, but in short it had to work. Something had to happen. I'm slowly seeing that the history of twentieth-century art is a bit of a fraud. It's not right. It's not actually about what the issues are. It will start disturbing those art historians – but it's going to happen, nevertheless.

PJ: Well, we're still talking about photography, but we're moving into a much more important area, really.

DH: It goes beyond it, way beyond it. I knew my photography was not just about pictures. I knew it took you into another area. That painting there [Hotel Acatlan*] is not about a hotel, it's about an attitude to space. And there is far more space in the picture than is normal, isn't there? And the longer you look, actually, the more you create space in your head because you're converting time to space. They are obviously interchangeable in our minds. Back and forth they go. And that's why we can't have a feeling of space without time. The idea that life was here and space then appeared, the old scientific idea, is dissolving. There's something very, very disturbing about these discoveries but something thrilling, I know that. Even in advertising they've realized that cubist photography can give you narrative, but they don't know how to deal with the rectangle of the page. These pictures don't finish up as rectangles. But you could adapt it. I'm going to do forty pages for French *Vogue*, without advertising. They said I could do what I want with it. I think they want me to make photographic experiments for the magazine. That's why I'm going to do it. You don't let that opportunity go, do you? You have to change things. And then you begin to change the world because you're changing the way you are perceiving. Your eye should be moving round all the time, all the time. Even while you acknowledge the space outside, you're still moving round in it. And it works. The longer you look, the more spatial it gets. That's how all these pictures work. And that must be like life.   [* see pages 96/7]

Mask made by the Fang, a Bantu people of West Africa. Given to Maurice Vlaminck who sold it to André Derain. It was certainly seen by Picasso and Matisse. George Braque said that 'Negro Masks opened up a new horizon for me'.
Drawing by Paul Joyce

PJ: And the advance of that work, as you've described it, over the earlier photographic work, particularly the Polaroids, is that, although you were moving all the time so that the backgrounds were represented properly, it was still according with a view of a room . . .

DH: Now, because it's so engrained in us, it's unbelievably hard to move away from it. It's taken me two years or more even to begin to realize that you should do it. But you then move into territory where you don't know at all what the space is going to look like. You've no idea. It's fascinating,

BaKota wooden figure covered with copper sheeting, usually placed above a package containing sample bones of memorable ancestors. Juan Gris made a cardboard copy of a similar funerary figure from Gambon to decorate his apartment.

because you then realize that you are beginning to make it yourself, creatively make it. The problem is that the rigid viewpoint is so fixed in us, that aspect of measurement is deeply fixed. It was not so with Picasso, and it's only in the last few years that I've looked at Picasso and realized that there's no distortion. None. Even in Bacon you think there is, because he's still got a traditional space around him which means you are distanced.

Last January I was in Paris with Celia. We went to a Watteau exhibition – beautiful – there was a little painting of a woman being powdered by her servant. It's called 'The Intimate Toilette' [*c. 1715*] – very pretty, a charming picture, beautifully painted. You feel the skin and the softness. Well, next day we went to the Beaubourg to see the Kahnweiler gifts, and there was a little Picasso in which you could see the front and back of a girl. Now, if you can see the front and back, it means that you, the viewer, are in the picture. You weren't in the Watteau, you were a voyeur, looking from a distance. Picasso has done something more complex. He's made us not voyeurs but participators. And that seems to me to be an incredible achievement, one that we can't go back on. It's more exciting and it makes the world more intimate by drawing us into it. I think that's what we've not fully grasped about Picasso.

We've now got an art world that's trying to say, 'modernism has gone: we're now into post-modernism'. Well, you look at post-modern pictures and, frankly, they are going back to the old way of seeing, aren't they? There's something wrong there. In short, modernism is far from over, it's only just begun. People are very quick to say: thank goodness that's gone! But they are wrong, deeply wrong, including a lot of serious art people! If painting is just painting to put on a wall – to use Picasso's phrase, 'mealy painting' – then it's not that important. But the other way it is incredibly important. And that's what all art was in the past, that's why it was important. It does make us see the world. And it's there for ever. You can't actually go back on it.

PJ: It changes your view of the world, and it changes your relationship to the world.

DH: Have you read *The Re-enchantment of the World*? Beautiful title, isn't it? Morris Berman. And, another great title, *Einstein's Space and Van Gogh's Sky*. And that's by two authors, I've forgotten their names right now. Also *The Dancing Wu Li Masters* is a very good introduction to quantum ideas. And you'll instantly see the connections with pictures. In fact, through what they consider to be metaphysics, a new picture of the world is emerging – wider perspectives, new horizons. They are thinking in metaphors which, I realize, apply naturally to pictures. *The Dancing Wu Li Masters* was written about seven years ago, it's witty and funny. I'd get that book first. He has a wonderful chapter about the philosophical implications of there being no neutral viewpoint.

La Toilette, c. 1717, by Jean-Antoine Watteau

London: September 1985

David was in London briefly in September 1985 and we arranged to meet at Kasmin's Knoedler Gallery in Cork Street. As the interruptions to our conversation there were constant, David suggested a change of scene, and so we repaired to Fortnum and Mason in Piccadilly. The noise level there was politely deafening. During the chat (over, as I recall, tripe and Guinness) David wanted to draw a perspective sketch to illustrate a point he was making. Having no pen to hand, he deftly extracted a cheap ballpoint from a passing waitress, who snatched it back a couple of minutes later, leaving David to complete his diagram in mid-air.

Later we moved on to Pembroke Studios where he showed me the new pieces he was working on for the forty-page section in Vogue. The massive joiner of the Place Furstenberg at first seemed surprisingly simple, almost a homage to Atget. On further examination its execution was anything but simple, and it made me hungry to see the whole magazine spread. A couple of days later David flew to Paris to finalize the design.

PJ: I've been looking at all we've said and it's fascinating. Speaking now, as a non-practising photographer, I think you've brought a great deal to photography through this work of yours. I would say you've expanded its consciousness. Is there anything that photography has taught you?

DH: When I began the experiments, about four and a half years ago, I had no idea that it would lead to what it did. So, it has taught me a great deal and that is its real value to me. Whether the photographs themselves are works of art, or whatever they are, frankly, I couldn't really care less. It's what it taught me. I was very excited when I began but, in fact, I'm only just realizing now how much it has opened up. It affects painting, it affects drawing, it affects your seeing and think-

ing. I've now given up the intense work on it. I've no doubt that I'll make some more pictures, but I'll only do them when I've thought it out more, and that will probably be from the painting. Painting can give you far, far more and I'm concerned about painting as a depiction of the visible world.

PJ: You've had a love-hate relationship with photography for over twenty years. There's obviously something about the camera which is deeply fascinating for you, isn't there?

DH: Yes, yes! But in 1982 I picked up the Polaroid camera just to play around with.

PJ: It's interesting that when you began seriously with the photographic experiments you chose the Polaroid. That's the one camera that works on the philosophy that it is possible to achieve a perfect single image.

DH: Well, the Polaroids led me to think that what was happening was very complicated, and virtually impossible without that particular camera, without being able to see the thing half-way through. The Polaroids were far more complex than any of the other pictures at first. But now the collages have got a lot more complex than the Polaroids could ever be. I don't fully know where it's leading. I do know that it's interesting, though. Of course, there are people who think I'm crazy, who think that I'm barking with madness! And that *tells* me something is going on.

Yet I realized, as the collages got more complex, that the physical surface they made had to be acknowledged and seen in a way that no ordinary photograph could be seen. The eye cannot always fully recognize the surface. It breaks through it, doesn't it? I was lucky to have the opportunity to do the *Vogue* piece, they just asked me at the right moment. They did say they had asked me two years before, but I'd ignored that; obviously I was too busy doing something else. This time when they asked me I realized what the opportunity

Painting used as the cover design for *Vogue* (Paris), edition no. 662, December 1985/January 1986

really was. All right, you can do things in a book, but that's not the same as doing forty pages in a magazine that's distributed merely as a magazine. It was a chance to make something physical. I assume people will keep the magazine, they won't actually throw it away, because they will know there's something slightly different about it. They might not understand how it's working, probably not many people will, but I'm sure they will *feel* it.

Also, I wanted to show that complex photographs could be printed on a page in a magazine. After all, if a photograph cannot be reproduced today, its effect will be slight, not many people will see it. Most photographs are simply reproduced in books – that's the way people see them. They are photographs of photographs, but the purists who say we should only see the real thing are putting it on a par with, say, some

select little watercolour group who show only to a few people. The strength of photography is that it can be reproduced without losing a great deal. The difference between seeing a very well-reproduced Cartier-Bresson in a book, and seeing the real print, I think is slight, whereas the difference between a real drawing and one reproduced in a book is quite different. The eye feels a different texture of paper, different marks, subtle colouring and so on that it cannot feel with the photograph. But a photograph of a photograph is indistinguishable from a photograph. Yet I knew the photographs I made were not like this. That's a fascinating philosophical aspect of it, isn't it? It leads you to all the philosophical problems of depiction, which I've always been fascinated by, always been dealing with.

In fact, I can see other artists now going into problems that

I went into about sixteen years ago. They have been held back because of their reliance on photographic images. It took me a long time to come out of it. There was a three- or four-year period when I made pictures with one-point perspective, and the one point was bang in the middle of the canvas. This was when I'd really gone into photography seriously and realized there was something deeply wrong. Backing away from it to get to reality was the beginning of a never-ending struggle.

Nevertheless, I've found much more satisfying solutions to the problems I set now because of the thinking that photography *forced* me to do. I was forced to investigate exactly how the photograph represents reality. I grasped fully that it must be an abstraction, and I realized why we had been confused by thinking it was not an abstraction. When you know that it is one, you can make better use of it. The later pictures, like the 'Place Furstenberg', would be very, very hard to make copies of. That one is thickly layered with photographs, sometimes one on top of another because I changed it so much. In a way, even that physicality gives it something which you feel. Before there might have been simple overlaps, now they are much more complex. We've decided not to let anyone else reproduce it, but to make big Cibachrome copies so that it's clearly a photograph of a photograph. So there's only one now, and I'll keep it, that's the solution.

PJ: I understand that you haven't sold any of the Polaroid work, and you've kept all the originals of the first state of the photocollages. I can see why you don't want to disperse them. By keeping them complete they constitute a body of work.

DH: At the moment they are dispersed, there are a few exhibitions of them, but I have kept everything, including all the original pieces that I put together, and it's a massive body of work. As I said, there are times when you're subsidizing an activity and as long as I can get the money from another source, paintings and prints, then I will keep the photographs together. If I sold them it would be hard ever to get them back. I don't fully know what they are, but all my instincts tell me to keep them together.

There is another book called *The Origin of Consciousness in the Breakdown of the Bicameral Mind*. It's based on the discoveries about a kind of split brain. The author suggests that consciousness, as we know it, is actually only about three thousand years old, which is not very old at all. Before that time people were in direct communication with nature, and they heard voices that directed them, there were prophets and so on. There is evidence from the Bible, quoting it; from Homer, quoting it; it says they heard voices, and that these were probably insights, extraordinary insights. He says they could have been coming from a part of the brain where there is an unaccounted space.

Whether his theory is wild or not, it's still fascinating to read because of the evidence. We tend to think that human beings evolved into their present state thousands of years ago. Well, of course, they couldn't have done that, if you think about it. So, what is going on? Now what's interesting there is the question 'Is consciousness a part of reality?' If it's not, how can one part of reality see another part? The quantum ideas begin to take you into the area where consciousness creates reality, in other words, that it is an illusion.

The other realization I've had, which any artist will tell you about, is that the flat surface is a very mysterious thing. Very simple, yet rather mysterious. What you can do on a flat surface is amazing. Physical reality comes through this flat surface of my eye (although it's actually curved, it's two-dimensional) and is converted by the mind into space and materiality. There must be some relation between this two-dimensionality – the sense of the eye – and the mystery of ordinary two-dimensional surfaces. I've always been fascinated by this – that's why I make pictures, and that's why I don't go in for sculpture. It also accounts for my interest in paintings of swimming pools, or paintings of a surface. Any pattern on water is a pattern on a thin film of the surface of the water, rather like the water that must be over your eye. I now see that a lot of my early pictures were all about this.

There's an early painting of mine with an elaborate frame around it, and in the painting there's a little man touching the four edges of the side, saying ,'Help!' He's trying to get out of the frame and edge. I can look at my early work in another way now. The work may be involved with the theatre, but the

Place Furstenberg, Paris, August 7, 8 and 9, 1985
(photographic collage)

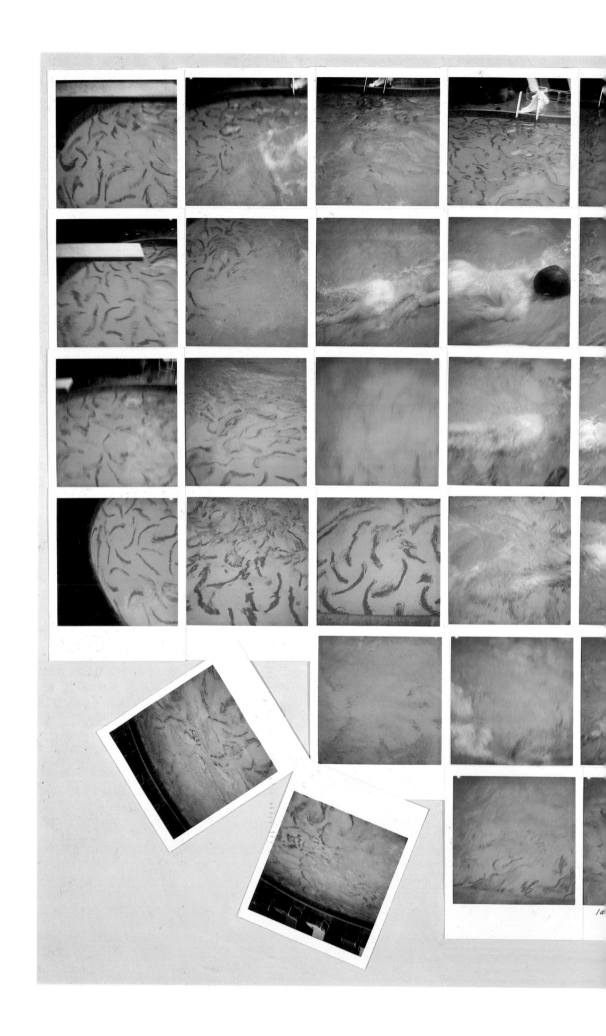

Ian Swimming, Los Angeles,
March 11th 1982
(Polaroid collage)

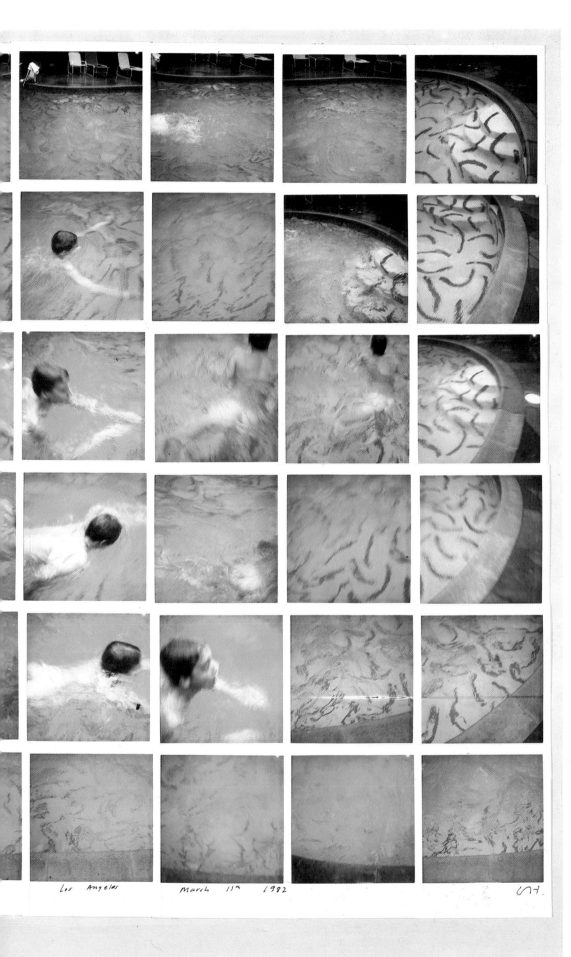

Los Angeles   March 11ᵗʰ 1982   D.H.

Play Within a Play, 1963
(oil on canvas with plexiglass)

theatre is deeply concerned with perspective too, and so it led me back to the same area.

PJ: When I left you last, you were talking about the depiction of the crucifixion, which you mentioned in a letter to Kitaj. At that point you were talking about the frozen eye, the moment of death, the relationship with photography, and the figure not moving, being pinned, like us, as spectators.

DH: This is speculative, of course – it's all it can be when there's no sure proof of it. I was struck, in Gombrich's book *Art and Illusion*, by the question 'Why did it take so long?' It's a rhetorical question, but he didn't really answer it. Well, why did it take so long for a book on perspective to be discovered, when his argument seems like an eternal truth? And the photograph confirms it. When I read that, I pondered this idea. Two or three years ago I talked about the camera obscura coming from Italy – that it was an Italian notion of looking at the world through a hole. But quite suddenly, last summer, I kept thinking about the crucifixion and how interesting it was. I now realize that you can't really have a horizontal meeting a vertical without stopping the eye dead.

PJ: So the graphic representation of perspective is very much like a crucifixion?

DH: In order to give the feeling of objects in space, they take away your body, and you become a theoretical point. It must be doing damage to us. Perspective, it dawned on me, makes narrative difficult. Narrative must be a flow in time and one-point perspective freezes time and space. If you look at the world through a hole, and fix your eye rigidly as well, you're going to kill yourself, aren't you?

Cézanne noticed what happened when you look with two eyes, and doubt where something is. There is a connection between that and the act of crucifying, which contains only one action. The action of beheading, or the arrow through the heart, is an action which means there's a moment of life and a moment of death. It's full of life one minute, and full of death the next. Crucifying is a slow death, and it's caused by lack of movement. Lack of movement is death: movement is life.

Crucifixion by Masaccio

That is clear, isn't it? The perspective picture brings us death. These connections seem so clear now, and nobody's written about them. They are our discovery.

PJ: And then you remember that the Renaissance artists were obsessed with the crucifixion. When they investigated those notions of perspective, that subject matter must have conjoined perfectly with their theories.

DH: They did. If Christ had been beheaded, the pictorial

representation of it would have been more difficult, wouldn't it?

PJ: Of course. And which moment do you choose?

DH: And it's all about suffering, isn't it? Bodily suffering, not just psychological suffering. Theologically, one can say that this was the first time that man had conceived God as a human being, which is, of course, on the road to saying, 'We are God'. That's part of the trouble. The idea of infinity was the God that died at the end of the nineteenth century. My idea of the God that's here now means we are part of him. It makes sense to me. You see then that the Renaissance was part of the movement of bringing the human being to God. But now, we have to get rid of that distance by seeing another way.

Cubism moved the viewer into the picture, pushing him, pulling him in. Well, it's by no means resolved. Probably it never will be, we've opened up something that will just go on in a most exciting way. Photography has to change. There are signs that it's beginning. If the people who make commercial photographs realize their photographs look dead, once they compare them with these, then they will start altering them. Dead photographs will make people think about this. It's exciting because it will lead all photographers to think a lot more deeply about their process – looking, seeing. The moment you've got twenty photographs to join up, you've got quite a complexity, haven't you? It's fascinating.

PJ: A computer couldn't give you those combinations. You'd go outside an ordinary numerical projection.

DH: Yes, the moment you get to fifty or sixty, and four corners, the number is gigantic, isn't it?

PJ: It's gigantic after ten or twelve in the way that you combine them. In commercial photography you can lay down the single thing that needs to be described – a hairstyle, six different ways; a car, six different ways. It's simple. But if you said to a photographer, who was using a large format camera: photograph Fortnum and Mason at lunch time in a new way, he wouldn't know where to begin. At the end of the day, he'd

shoot a million rolls and he wouldn't know how to put it together. You've got to be an artist to actually cope with that. It's difficult enough to be an artist as good as *you* are and be able to cope with it, isn't it?

DH: Yes. If *I* found it very difficult, then everybody else certainly will. Well, nobody could do it more quickly. Nobody. There's no way I know of. And there's not that many people who are willing to spend that kind of concentration and time on one particular piece.

PJ: Certainly not photographers, because they haven't got that built into their consciousness . . .

DH: They are not used to it, no.

PJ: An artist may take a week to do a picture, or two weeks or a month, but I reckon each work of yours takes a week to put together.

DH: I must tell you that the British Embassy one took me three weeks. The one of Christopher Isherwood in the house talking with Bob went into three versions before I got it right. And each time what I was doing was re-doing the drawing. That took longer, far longer, because I knew I wasn't happy. It didn't feel like space. Finally, the third time, I got it to work. Frankly, it was lying there for over a month.

In my letter to Kitaj I spoke about sounding space . . .

PJ: You mentioned that in relation to your improved hearing . . .*

DH: But I believe that if you go deaf, you must develop a finer visual sense of space. The trouble is that unless you were expressing this in some way, nobody would ever know. You can't describe it in words. You have to express it visually. And I think there's a lot in that, because the moment I got the second ear fixed, space became spatial again . . . Sound also is spatial. It gives us a sense of space, doesn't it? If you were blind, you would develop whatever kind of hearing you've got spatially. You know directions of sounds. If somebody speaks to you from over there, that's the direction you would

---

* Hockney had been having problems with his hearing.

Christopher Isherwood talking to Bob Holman, Santa Monica, March 14th, 1983 (detail of Don Bachardy) (photographic collage)

Luncheon at the British Embassy,
Tokyo, February 16th, 1983
(photographic collage)

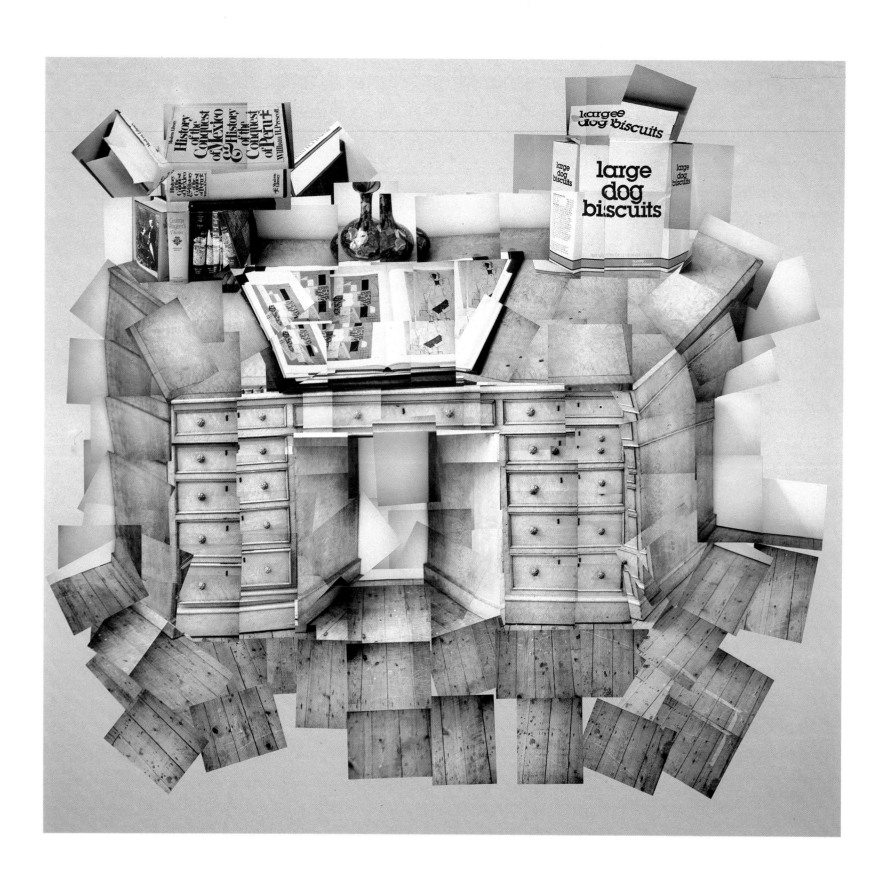

The Desk, July 1st, 1984
(photographic collage)

walk in. So your hearing would be used to define space a great deal. Well, obviously we can do this. I just added this as a kind of postscript, really, but I think there's a lot in it. It made me very much more aware of space, and my work is often about space.

PJ: You've moved through photography to a different kind of drawing and painting, but you picked up a camera, which would seem to be the least likely object to help you with space!

DH: Well, the joiners ultimately make the camera a drawing instrument, and so you're back to drawing as a very important thing. Whereas the camera was seen as the destroyer of drawing, wasn't it? Now, *that* was a mistake ...

PJ: But there's something a camera *can* do, and certainly in *your* hands. Look at the desk picture – what it represents is the surface of the desk in a way that would take you weeks to paint, if you wanted the desk to look that way.

DH: In painting you can do it another way. You wouldn't bother doing the exact surface that way, but the camera catches it, so that's what you use. When you take a camera close to the desk you can show the wood, it gives that strong illusion. But the stronger illusion, which you can realize fully, is that you are connected with the desk, and the whole world is connected, the universe is connected. This is opposed to the idea that we are separate from it.

PJ: But have we found there a photographic strength, do you think, which is that, in texture, in detail, the camera can record the way we know things to be?

DH: The camera can record light on to surfaces wonderfully, but it can describe as well. Description is subjective, it describes that desk and, therefore, connects you with it. The description means the desk is not on its own, there is a describer involved. Again, we're back to the participator, not the observer. And to say that the camera can do that as well then involves it in drawing, and that would upset a lot of things. And I think what will happen ultimately is – in another ten or fifteen years – that the ordinary photograph

will begin to have a primitive look to it. Most people would not think so now, when it seems the least primitive of pictures. That's exciting as well, because you can only make a picture look primitive if you've made more complex ones. When you look at the *Rossignol* photograph I made and compare it to the earlier ones, they look flat by comparison, don't they? Absolutely, totally flat. But no artist sees his work as separate, the ideas are continuous, they go through into everything. I'm sure not that many people figure it out – you have to do a bit of work. Most people are probably just enjoying it, apart from the *Guardian* critic! Well, I don't mind that, I think now one should expect opposition. The opposition will be ignorant; I don't think there could be an intelligent opposition to these ideas.

PJ: How can there be, when you're telling the truth, David?

DH: When I first showed these photographs in New York, some woman in the *Village Voice* said: he's done it all wrong. Well, you make an experiment to learn something, it's not a question of right or wrong. They are looking at it in a wrong way if they say that, to begin with. You must put it down to ignorance. I don't mind. The criticism of modern art was always from an ignorant viewpoint. And I don't think that has gone away, even among people who think they know about modern art, or write for the *Guardian*. I don't think we should expect anything else.

PJ: I don't think we should even take account of it, really.

DH: No, but it's interesting that it should still go on, after eighty years!

PJ: But they're a generation behind you anyway. They always will be. The artist, by definition, is way ahead and they are going to take some time to catch up. There's a wonderful description you made of colour in photography, you spoke about the fugitive nature of colour.

DH: It was to do with the piece I did at Bradford – I kept adding the photographs each day. It was the first piece made without the photographs all having been taken at once. Finally the third day, when I wanted to add more, the lab that

Bradford, Yorkshire,
July 18, 19, 20th, 1985
(photographic collage)

we'd used closed, so we took them to an ordinary one-hour photo place, and they made them all blue. They dealt in holiday snaps, and they made Bradford look like the South of France. And the people watching me construct it were horrified that I was going to add them to the others. And I said it didn't matter. And in the end they *were* amazed; they said, you know, it actually *doesn't* matter. You know then that it was at a different time, and you know also that it was a different process. The idea of getting the colour right comes from the belief that there's a fixed colour out there. Well, of course, there isn't.

PJ: It's as right as the print before!

DH: But the argument is not about colour. The idea of there being a true colour would mean that colour is separate from everything. It's the old idea of separation. It all becomes irrelevant. As the colours fade, there will still be a lot there. They don't fade completely away; you don't suddenly have blank paper, there's always something there. Of course the line won't fade, and the photograph is deeply about line. I never worried about colour. You might prefer one to the other sometimes, just for your own pleasure. But the idea that it was all fixed separate from you is nonsense. Many good ideas have a simplicity about them, but underneath there's a complexity. Einstein's theory of relativity has a wonderful simplicity about it, but a complex pattern to get there. If the idea is merely complex and there is no simplicity, then there's something wrong probably. I'll tell you a good book that would add to this – a book on mathematics which I couldn't put down. But it is for the layman – there are no equations in it. It's called *Beyond Infinity – the Human Side of Mathematics*. Read it. You'll see all the connections as I did. It's fascinating. The reading stimulates you and confirms your instincts. And it's thrilling that this happens. I must have read thirty books on the subject – science, physics, psychology. And it all comes back to simple but complex ideas.

PJ: You'll obviously do some major photographic work in Paris next week, won't you?

DH: I'm going to make the *Vogue* issue fun and attractive – I have to do that, that's my way. There is something serious about it, but I can't help it, I have to put the charm in. Somebody else might not, but I can't really go against my own nature. Artists can't do that. You have to accept it. But if I can make the *Vogue* piece work it will be even better than the book of photographs because it will show how these things can be adapted. You're forced to bring drawing back in order to make photographs that way. And if a photographer thinks it would be better to know rudimentary things about drawing, he can be taught. You can't teach somebody to draw like Picasso or Matisse, but you can teach people to draw quite competently, and at least get the principles. There are principles involved when dealing with a flat surface, and they are not difficult to teach, but they've stopped teaching them because they thought they weren't necessary. They thought the photograph was doing it. Suddenly you could get the art schools incredibly lively again because drawing would apply to departments they thought had nothing to do with it. The more you know about drawing the better, if you're connected to anything visual. After all, Cartier-Bresson can draw rather well. I'm sure that's why he makes wonderful photographs. He understands the principles of pictorial space.

And Annie Leibovitz started as a painter, she knows a little bit about drawing. I think one of the main things that has emerged is the idea that there is a difference between abstraction and representation. After all, a lot of serious people think there's a difference. But in the direction I'm going there isn't one. I can't help but come up against this – *anything* on a flat surface is an abstraction. And it's the fact that one particular abstraction of reality is regarded as a very, very vivid depiction of it that causes problems in other areas. A little art problem expands into an area that's a lot bigger than you thought. I realize now that not many people have gone on this path, and a lot of people think I'm quite crazy. But I think I'm absolutely on the right line – I sense it, I feel it. Now, I'm just staying here, I'm not travelling. Everything tells me to stay put and work, work at it.

New York:
November 1985

In November 1985 I flew to New York for the International Emmy Awards as one of my films, Summer Lightning, *had made it to the final selection. David was there at the same time for the re-staging of* Parade *at the Metropolitan Opera.*

One evening in the Mayflower Hotel David produced the page proofs of the forthcoming Christmas edition of French Vogue – forty pages of extraordinary new work, conceived and executed to fit into the existing magazine format, but with revolutionary concepts of reverse perspective, 'bleeding' pictures right to the edges, and objects reproduced on the page to their actual size. As a considered statement of his current preoccupations, these pages seemed to me to be masterly. They showed a great artist adapting to a medium and transforming it. Three months after publication this issue had become a collector's item.

David told a story about the Metropolitan's production of Parade; *how all the kids in the New York staging are tough little pros, in sharp contrast to the well-mannered Home Counties set in the Glyndebourne production. (The American kids make their parents rich doing TV commercials.) During the New York rehearsals two hardened 11-year-old troupers were overheard talking backstage. One turned to the other in disbelief and said, 'Look at that, a* red *tree.' The other shrugged and replied, 'That's nothing, wait until you see the designer!'*

Apart from such flashes of characteristic humour, David seemed abstracted and distant on this visit. Several of his friends were ill, and one was actually dying in a New York hospital. His relief at the prospect of returning to Los Angeles was apparent; he looked drained and exhausted. Our conversations appeared to offer him a temporary distraction. We agreed our work was still not done.

PJ: I'm very interested in abstraction and representation – photography, particularly, seems to be totally representational. What you see is what you recognize. A detail of your desk brings you right up close to the desk. So photography, particularly, has that tension built in.

DH: I'll tell you one thing that's happening. In Los Angeles there are a number of film processes that are coming to the fore – they might call them special effects and so on, but people will say to me that there are landscapes that a computer can make *and it looks real!* And I say: you mean it looks real in a *perspective* way. They have techniques now, whereby on a film a man could look as though he's walking around a very grand room which he never actually walked around. The superimposition of one image on to another in an honest way would be collage: in a dishonest way, when you take away the glue so that it doesn't look like a collage, it is actually what's happening a great deal on television and in films. Now, there's a side of all this that's Stalinist, in a sense. You could have, on a TV screen, a picture of somebody who looked as though he were sitting at a White House dinner, and you'd think he was actually there. He'd probably never been near it. It could be made to look quite authentic, even on a newsreel. This is cunning. It's going to be so easy to do. My point is that it's easy to do in an old picture, but it would not be easy to do in a cubist picture. Not at all. You'd recognize superimposition. You can recognize where that's leading. There are political implications in this, aren't there? Well, I've joked before that if you had cubist television you'd see Ronald Reagan reading the cue-cards because you could see round the corner. And, in a way, that's perhaps what we really need. I see it as a joke. People again will say that it's David's outrageous silly joke. But there's an element of it that's not a joke.

I got through the mail the other day a process from a firm in New York. It's a process of superimposing images. And they

Political manipulation. Czechoslovak Party leader
Alexander Dubček with President Svoboda

After his expulsion from the Communist Party
he was 'painted out', while Svoboda was enlarged

sent an example – the Cast Iron Building with lightning
striking it and the top bits falling off, and so on. Now, it only
looks good if you think what an ordinary photograph looks
like. Of course, it couldn't work with my method. An
ordinary photograph (or even television) is going about
abstraction in a most deceitful and manipulative way. Now
that deceit lays open possibilities for political manipulation.
For how long, I don't know. Stalin's technique of taking
Trotsky out of the photograph did make some people think
for a little while that Trotsky was not at Lenin's side. But, of
course, after a while, they learned about retouching photographs, and so the technique couldn't work any more. People
learned to doubt the photograph that way. Well, the biggest
doubts now are going to come because of these techniques.
How will you know that anything you see is real? The
unhealthy side of this is that people fall for it; the healthy side
is that people realize that it is merely an abstraction. It's like
war on TV in a way. It is seen as a kind of game. You're never
involved, it's just on a screen and you're playing with it. The
trouble is that the people who are putting out the pictures
think that TV is reality.

PJ: Well, they're abstracting themselves from it!

DH: A great deal of the media has a vested interest in an old
way of seeing. I'm not suggesting people are evil, because I
don't think too many people have thought it out. There are a
lot of innocent people involved. It could be that any image
you see could be made up of twenty images and you don't
know it. That is the deceit. Maybe people don't think it's
reality on TV. Maybe they see the whole thing as enter-
tainment, including the news, or what they say is news.
Maybe that's the only way they can take what is there. Every
night there must be a hundred people killed on TV. Well, in
the past people didn't see a hundred people killed every
evening, did they? What do you think it might do to us? Well,
our defence is that they are actors; they just get up. Oh, he
was killed last Monday as well!

The only kind of TV I've realized is fascinating and grip-
ping is life. Now, if it's life, something else is there. That *now*
corresponds to my *now*. The only things that are live on TV
are sports events, because nobody wants to see a non-live
sports event. They don't want to see last week's football
match, when they know what happened. It would hardly be
exciting. I think it does make a difference: I remember watching Prince Charles's wedding, and I actually stayed up in L.A.
because it was great television. It was happening at that time.

The Hitch-hiker, 1983 (photographic collage)

I wasn't interested in seeing a film of it later. It had to be at that time, i.e. now. There's only now. Television is deeply involved in pictorial problems, even though the directors think they're not – they just point the camera and think that's it. There are many other implications, some that people want to avoid. They don't want to know. And it's interesting, even now, watching the news about Libya – you get pictures purporting to be live, as though it were not rehearsed and put on for the camera. In short, you're back to the old position of the fake fly on the wall. Frankly, I don't believe any of them. I think it's all a kind of TV game. It would be dangerous if you thought you could rely on these images and what they said. Not that you know the truth from the newspapers! But these are moving images, and it looks as if it's now, they tell you that it's live – '*Live from the White House*'!

PJ: In a way, the camera's become the arch-enemy. The old one-point perspective, personified now in the movie camera, has led people to *believe*, particularly with film and now with television, which is just a second-rate version of film.

DH: You must know about it because you've worked in film and TV. About six months ago – they asked me if I'd like to use some new equipment. They showed me how they had a guy doing something on a set in a studio. But then with this projection behind he appeared to be on a bridge with a school bus approaching, and he had to jump out of the way. I saw him jump in front of me in the studio, but on the screen it looked as though he was on the bridge, jumping out of the way of a bus. Very authentic-looking. There were no seams to it. In a way, it was very, very good. But whereas Fellini's stylizations are honest, these others are not. 'Stalin's technique' does come apart because we've learned about it. The moment people watching TV images know how it's done, they won't believe any image at all.

PJ: A lot of artists today have been caught in this maelstrom of film, photography and video. They need to deal with what they think is reality, or what they think people want to see. For the most part I think that the work, not the work of original film-makers like Fellini or Nic Roeg but of artists,

has been pretty disappointing when they turn to this new technology. What is interesting now is that more people go to see the great artists of the past – Matisse, Van Gogh, or whoever. There's more interest in prophetic statements now than there ever has been in the history of art. There is something to be learned from this, I think.

DH: People are certainly more visually literate than they used to be. It is said there are too many images, but in fact people are just repeating them. It doesn't matter how many images are made the old way, there are always going to be too many! But there are never too many of the new kind. The idea that new images can possibly come out of old seems naive to me. Of course you can get poetic conjunctions of things. Poetry happens, whether in film, or television or on a flat surface. It's always difficult to know what the true art of our time is.

I see that Mr Saatchi made a catalogue quite recently, called 'The Art of Our Time' – a pretty arrogant title. He obviously thinks he knows what it is. I don't think we do. The picture now is a bit too jumbled for us to see. It takes a little time to sort out. There was a piece in the *L.A. Times* on Sunday about the Oscars, pointing out that loads of the great, great Hollywood people never got Oscars, including Laurel and Hardy, Charlie Chaplin and so on. Well, somehow the middle-brow can never see certain things are serious. They couldn't see Laurel and Hardy as serious art; they saw them as low comedy. But they have survived to be regarded now as serious art. The idea that you know what's significant in art right now, in art that's just been done, is ridiculous. You'd have to be superhuman to know and understand what was most significant.

PJ: Maybe there's so much happening with apparently new ways of representing the world that we can't stand back and say what is good and bad within that. The mix of things is more complicated than it ever was. The choice for artists is simply amazing. Do they go into video, do they go into film, do they use the existing photographic images to make their own statements? I feel that this has more to do with a television culture than an artistic sensibility. I don't see how television can change one's image of the world. All it can do is apparently show you more things happening at once. But then, we always knew that things were happening simultaneously, didn't we?

DH: Yes, but television is becoming a collage – there are so many channels that you move through them making a collage yourself. In that sense, everyone sees something a bit different.

PJ: So, the man sitting at home is his own artist.

DH: Well, if he sees it that way, but he might perceive it rather awkwardly, thinking: where's that programme I really want? What's all this stuff in the way? Whereas somebody a little more contemplative will enjoy the journey.

PJ: You know they are going to have television soon where all sixteen channels are showing at the same time.

DH: Yes, well that's collage, isn't it? Collage is the key, the key to break perspective. What I call deceitful collage will do a lot of damage first, but it will fail eventually. The cubists were the first to realize what the invention was, and it's very powerful, a lot more powerful than you think. It's not just a decorative thing.

Los Angeles: April 1986

In April 1986 I returned to Los Angeles with a crew to shoot two hour-long films on Hollywood in the seventies. I spent several evenings with David. This was my first introduction to his Xerox work, which was being treated most suspiciously by his friends and business colleagues, gallery owners and the like. He had just acquired a small Canon machine and was excited by the fact that you could change the colour with ease. It was merely a matter of slipping out one cartridge, then inserting another. So it was perfectly possible to lay a background in black, change the cartridge and overlay a red area, and then do the same with a green. During my visit I saw his studio turn into an artist's impression of one of those large copy-shops, with people running around at breakneck speed as if trapped in an old silent movie.

One day we had time off from filming, so I arranged to visit David in the early morning, around 9 a.m., so we could talk before he started work. I arrived to find him quite distracted. He had woken in the middle of the night and couldn't get back to sleep. 'Got something on my mind . . .' he muttered, leading the way to the studio. I knew then that our interview was not going to happen, but I wouldn't have missed the day, for I was able to see him working flat-out on a complex six-part Xerox piece. He began by sketching the design across six separate sheets of A4-sized paper, then would concentrate on one of those, using the basic design as a 'master' and feeding additions through the Canon photocopier so that the original was gradually overlaid. Thus a design was built up through a number of different 'states', not unlike conventional work on a lithographic plate, but at a hugely increased speed. He worked from 10 a.m. to 6 p.m. without a break, finishing each master design to his satisfaction, then doing an edition of sixty from each sheet. Three hundred and sixty original Hockneys, designed and printed in one day!

David believes that photocopying machines, and the next generation of laser printers, will revolutionize publishing and

printing. Artists will be able to produce and edit work entirely from within their own studios, as indeed writers will be able to publish their work via desktop computers. The electronic age has caught up with traditional methodology, bringing the concept of the 'Global Village' one step closer. The artist in his ivory tower will no longer be isolated. Technology has brought the world to his workbench.

That evening we moved through to the newly constructed kitchen which now forms part of his living room, by the terrace overlooking the pool. Any thoughts of relaxing and reaching for the tape recorder were soon dispelled as he flung himself into preparations for dinner. His approach to cooking, which he is very good at and enjoys hugely, has the same single-mindedness that he brings to any other task. His only moment of hesitation was over the broccoli. 'How long does it need?' he asked. 'About six minutes,' I replied. 'Right,' he said, thrusting a wicked-looking kitchen knife at me, 'get cutting!' I sighed, abandoned all thoughts of photography, chopped the broccoli and had one of the best dinners of my life. Next day we were able to get back to the conversations.

DH: The photography did take me back to painting. Since the *Vogue* piece I haven't done any new photographs. Nevertheless, I think that piece helped a lot. Many people understood what I was saying because within that magazine there was the contrast between one way of seeing and another. I've realized when I give lectures, for example, people react in very positive ways. They recognize to a certain extent what I'm saying, but I'm not sure they see it. I see it, of course, but I think it's hard for other people, isn't it?

PJ: Yes, I think there is a surface understanding, which you can explain, but if you go beyond that it's almost like penetrating the surface of reality. You have gone well beyond any

Dancing Flowers, May 1986 (six panels)
(Home Made Xerox print(s))

ordinary notions of perspective, which leaves us looking and perhaps understanding what you've done without necessarily acquiring the language to do it ourselves. I've always felt this was a problem with what you were doing. You used to say: well, it won't be long before they're all doing it. However, I think that point is further off now, because you've gone much further than you had done two years ago when we first started talking.

DH: Yes, I've gone a lot further.

PJ: For example, the *Vogue* piece of your work trolley is apparently simple but in fact is infinitely complex. The truth is, if one tries to follow in an artist's footsteps, how can one expect in reality to come to the same destination? Just because one has the same camera as the artist uses, does one really expect to achieve the same results?

DH: Even the Xerox machine tells me this. I've also come to realize the camera is merely a medium. A machine is just a medium. You can use them, they all have a kind of individuality. But you don't have to use the machine in a mechanical way. It's interesting that this work has taken me back to look at Oriental art. At the Los Angeles County Museum of Art, there are two shows which you must see now! The one you go into first is a collection of Japanese pictures that has been given to the County Museum, quite a large collection with some beautiful things in it. I must have spent at least an hour and a half in there. Wonderful, marvellous things of monkeys and so on, based on observation; you really feel close to everything. Now when you come out of this you go into an exhibition of landscapes by George Inness, not a bad nineteenth-century American landscape painter. The moment I went into the room, I felt a cringe, I *cringed* because the paintings (quite unlike the Japanese ones) made the world seem over *there*. I was separate from the paintings, I felt that the picture was a window that he had gone into and I was outside it. It was very pronounced, for me. You go and see if it doesn't work on you that way. It is a profound difference – one is the belief that the world is out there, and the other one is the belief that the real world is inside us.

PJ: So the hand and the brain are connected, and not dispassionate observers.

DH: That's it.

PJ: What I got out of the books which you suggested I read, those dealing with quantum physics or new notions of scientific investigation, was that there is a fundamental difference now, with the 'New Science', which is that the observer in an experiment is not an objective and quite uninvolved person...

DH: He's a participator...

PJ: And this in turn changes the nature of the experiment. Have I read that correctly?

DH: Yes, you have.

PJ: I'd like you to explain the relationship of this to your current work.

DH: The question really is to do with the observer and the observed. George Inness represents the division between these. In Japanese art they are more together. Science now says they are together, doesn't it? The other system did work for a long time, but it can't work now. It's parallel, it can't be merely accidental that the same problem is one of depiction as well. The photograph must represent the old materialistic view of the world in the sense that perspective is about a view of the world in which objects are separate from you. My point about the desk photograph was that if you are seeing around the corners of the desk, you are seeing yourself move. It isn't just the desk, it is you and the desk. You are united with it, in the process of looking. You are aware of yourself in space. Have you read *The Aquarian Conspiracy* by Marilyn Ferguson? The book is about revolutions happening now, and it's about the philosophical implications of recent discoveries and their relevance to consciousness, awareness, and so on. It's fascinating, written by a journalist, and it's quite readable, not difficult at all. She's very bright and she is linking all kinds of manifestations to do with these themes. It's about our expanding consciousness as science takes us towards mysticism and meditation, things that can probably bring us closer to reality. I can understand it because I can understand it within myself. This is why I have decided to cut myself off here and pursue the ideas now locked away in my mind. That's why I don't want to travel very much.

PJ: You read quantum physics extensively for about nine months. What did that bring you?

DH: I did grasp some things, but they were simply the parallels to my own enquiries. I instantly recognized parallels, and therefore I felt very confident. I realized the implications for depiction. Well, I've always been fascinated by depiction, and its problems. I know the only people who are interested in this are certain kinds of painters. Photographers have not been that interested in the problems of depiction because they thought it had all been settled for them – the issue of perspective, for instance. Photographers felt it couldn't be their problem, it was built into their work, and therefore had to be accepted. Well, it's not accepted. That's what I discovered. And if you suddenly find it's not, something's opened wide.

PJ: Were there any particular quantum investigations about the nature of the physical world and matter which struck particular chords in you?

DH: Well, when you read about the search for the smallest particle and so on, you begin to realize that it's the search for infinity – a never-ending quest. But matter is not the ultimate reality. Matter is simply made up of energy, that's what they say. Our consciousness has a great deal to do with this energy – after all, there is matter *here* in our brains. Scientists are looking into this, it's an area they're fascinated with. You see it takes you where science hasn't been before, it moves into psychic areas, doesn't it? The materialist view which dominated for three or four hundred years, and is still powerful today, was the commonly held view. Well, it's only when the commonly held view is changed that we can move to another awareness. But it begins with just a few people, that's what *The Aquarian Conspiracy* is about. The lifted awareness of the few leads to many following later. Of course there is a time lag.

There is one problem they are coming up against now. The photograph can now be altered on the computer. You must have seen it. The Pyramids can be moved closer together. Of course, it doesn't mean that the Pyramids *are* closer together; you move them an inch in a depiction on a flat surface, that's all. Nevertheless this can only work with an ordinary perspective photograph. Cubist photography says that you are not sure what the distances between the Pyramids are. The other way says there is a fixed distance, and we can now alter it. Now that seems to me to be taking us further from reality, whereas the cubist idea is taking us towards it. They now have movies which use computer-made landscapes, and they say they look real! They are only real in the context of the perspective picture we are used to. We must use the computer another way.

PJ: The way it's used must rely on the programmer.

[After an interval]

PJ: Do you think that photography can tell us anything more about the physical world?

DH: Not really, it couldn't get close enough. I've no doubt that strong images will be made, although I must tell you that I was reading a review of a biography of Robert Capa, and I learned that the famous photograph of the soldier in the Spanish Civil War was posed. Well, something collapses there. The image is there, but a certain authenticity that made it into something has gone, hasn't it? Did you know it was posed?

PJ: I knew there was controversy about it, that some people denied it hotly and others said it was clearly fabricated. Yes, it always worried me, because I thought that Capa was a great war photographer and achieved magnificent results. But that took away the bite, the reality, what one thought was a reality. It plays then with the notion of what is real.

DH: It's always the same thing we come back to, isn't it? But collage is happening, and I'm concerned about it being honest. It is happening.

PJ: Well, perhaps Capa's was an honest collage?

Work Trolley, 1985
(photographic collage)

DH: Of course, the very fact that the image has done a great job leads you to ask why it matters whether it's real or not? I remember seeing a film with Marcello Mastroianni about the French Revolution, about two or three years ago. There's a scene where the French Revolutionary mob comes to attack. But the director and cameraman quite rightly don't spend too long on their faces because they don't look hungry, because they don't look like peasants who have nothing to eat. You might put clothes on which suggest that, but you can't make faces do that, and make-up cannot do that. If you saw a newsreel of the Revolution, even if you had posed it, if it was happening at the time with these people it would be revealed in their faces.

PJ: So we are saying that photography, in the sense of a portrait in its own time, has truth?

DH: Well, you can't escape your own time. No way. If I tried to make what I regarded to be an exact copy of a Rembrandt, even brush-stroke for brush-stroke, I couldn't help putting into it the twentieth-century view of Rembrandt. By the twenty-first century they would know that it was a twentieth-century copy of Rembrandt, just as we do with the nineteenth-century copies.

PJ: But looking back, particularly at photographs, it always strikes me that it's of sociological interest how a street looks, how people dressed, how they behaved one to another.

DH: Well, all old photographs *become* interesting, no matter who took them, aesthetics aside. There has been no end of photographs taken, and the vast majority are of humble people, but if any of them survive five hundred years they will be of great interest, not just to scholars, but to everybody. The

future won't separate the pin-up from Cartier-Bresson. The first is attempting to depict the nude in a certain way, it's reflecting certain things about our time. *Anything* five hundred years old is of interest to us. We might think the nude is trash now, but the future will decide that.

PJ: I think of that great photographer August Sander, who we mentioned once before, who did that wonderful series of portraits of Germans, I think around the time of the First World War...

DH: In the twenties and thirties.

PJ: Yes, that's right. Well, are those going to be judged as masterpieces of August Sander in two hundred years, or are they going to be seen as a fantastic document which happened to be gathered by him?

DH: August Sander saw it as a document, and then later it's seen as the work of August Sander, but eventually, I suppose, it will be seen as it was meant to be, as a document that August Sander did. But what is interesting is the document.

PJ: Absolutely. It's a very interesting notion that photography can't escape its own time.

DH: No, it can't, no matter what it tries to do.

PJ: But, then, doesn't a Van Gogh escape its own time?

DH: Nobody does.

PJ: But we still marvel at the Van Gogh, knowing that he didn't sell a picture, knowing that nobody gave a shit about him at the time, because of something which is timeless about the quality, the vision of it.

DH: Yes, there is something universal there, and we will respond for ever to that.

PJ: I'm beginning to believe through all these conversations, David, that no photographer is going to survive a century hence, as a so-called artist.

DH: No, probably not.

PJ: Apart from an artist who picks up the camera, which is a different thing. And all this hoo-ha about them really tells us more about the paucity of art than it does about photography as a great medium of expression.

DH: The debate has never been settled – 'Is it art or is it photography?' I don't think it ever will be. There's a cutting here from Australia about my photographs, saying they weren't art.

PJ: They say that your work isn't art?

DH: It says, 'They are photographs, this isn't art.' As if you have to pay duty on them, or something!

PJ: What's interesting is that about twenty-five or thirty years ago, people stopped asking that question, as if it had suddenly magically been answered. Before that, there was a big debate, is it art or not? And suddenly everybody in the photographic establishment, and in the art world, accepted that photography is art. But, you're right, it's never been properly engaged.

DH: The Australians are very conservative. They think that a photograph has to be just a mechanical reproduction of reality, but art must be an interpretation. That's what they think.

PJ: If someone was about to pick up a camera, someone who you thought was maybe a promising artist, or had some special vision or gift, is there any advice that you would give?

DH: Ask questions. That's what I'd say. When problems arise, ask yourself questions.

PJ: And don't expect the camera to answer them for you? What you've shown, I think, is that the camera raises more questions than it answers. But, ultimately, they are questions about oneself, aren't they? They aren't questions about the world, or art. It's almost as if the camera points back at you, when you pick it up. What are you going to do with this? What do you see? Can you see where photography might take you?

Spanish Loyalist at the Instant of Death
photograph by Robert Capa, 1936

DH: There will come a time when I'll suddenly decide: yes, I'll make another photograph. At the moment I've no reason to, so I'll wait till...

PJ: Till the moment comes?

DH: Yes.

PJ: What I've noticed in the photographic work, because that is the work that I've followed closely, is that you throw yourself into a piece, and then you stand back and think about it very hard, and then you do it again, and again, and maybe again. It seems to go through this constant process of throwing a punch and then stepping back to observe the effect before you move into action again. Can you see a time when the thought and the action might part, and you become all action?

DH: Well, that's happening now, apart from when I'm talking to you! Today and tomorrow I'm just working on painting. I'm not thinking it out, I'm just acting on ideas. It's with a brush I'm talking to myself now.

PJ: There's something about photography which is almost irrevocable, isn't there? You set up, shoot the picture, and that's it. Either you've got it, or you haven't. And if you haven't got it, you're fucked. For you making a picture is a process of getting to know, coming to terms with, moving around, exploring, relating to something that you're looking at. You have dispensed with the idea of the irrevocable picture, the one image that either captures it or doesn't. And I remember saying, in a piece that I wrote about you, that you could actually end up photographing the whole world because where *do* you stop? So that is the question, David, where do you stop?

DH: Well, you never stop. I never stop...

New York:
September 1986

On 12 September 1986 I returned to New York for an opening of David's photographic work at the International Center for Photography. This could be regarded as the storming of a bastion, and I had to be there to see it. ICP is run by Cornell Capa, brother of the late Robert Capa, one of the greatest photojournalists. The opening was a triumph, and my impression was that the American photographers approached the show with a greater openness than their English counterparts. They were genuinely interested, engaged and moved. This was a key exposure not only to photographers, but to artists, Madison Avenue executives, and television and film people.

Next morning I was in David's hotel room for an 8.30 a.m. meeting. I'd spent most of the night working on the manuscript. All he had on were underpants, hearing aid and a fag. We proceeded to talk about everything but the manuscript. He spoke of his growing disenchantment with England and the British. He had decided to abandon Pembroke Studios as any kind of working base in future and to use it only for a night or two when he had to visit London. He feels at home only in the North of England, when he joins his family for Christmas and other personal celebrations.

Our talk continued in the hotel coffee shop. In the corner, not far away, a throw-back to the sixties with long hair and paint-bespattered jeans sat with a sketch book in hand. His eyes lit on David's golden thatch and out came the crayons. I could see the 'artist' out of the corner of my eye, and sensed the possibility of an embarrassing incident. After a few minutes he sidled over and I let out a silent scream. He thrust the sketch under David's nose. It was truly dreadful, only the blond hair being in any way recognizable. 'What do you think, man?' David looked quizzical and concentrated hard on the drawing. 'Want to buy it?' David raised an eyebrow. 'It's for materials, man, they're sure expensive now.' Immediately David handed him a twenty-dollar bill. The guy nearly fell over. 'Hey, are you some kind of artist, man?' David nodded. 'Yeah, takes one to know one.' David held on to the drawing, and the guy reluctantly backed away. David placed the sketch under his chair. I said, 'It was the materials, wasn't it?' 'Of course,' replied David. 'We all need those.'

We talked another two hours away, until his 'limo' slid up to the hotel's entrance, and it seemed that we were still talking into the tape recorder as a phalanx of friends, relatives and assistants swept him into the smoked-glass interior.

PJ: Talking of your new work, you said something very interesting to me: it's changed again ... You didn't say: I'm seeing more. You made it something outside yourself. I found that fascinating, as if you were an objective observer of what you're creating.

DH: Well, I don't make that many of these large joiners now. They are very slow and I only tend to do them if I can push them in some interesting way. Otherwise I'd rather paint and draw. Doing that picture* I realized that it had gone further than any of the other pictures. The picture of the Place Furstenberg, which was in *Vogue*, took about four days' work just to draw the space. I thought at the time it was pretty complex, but of course the Place Furstenberg is a small confined space.

But 'Pearblossom Highway' shows a crossroads in a very wide open space, which you only get a sense of in the western United States. Obviously a large, wide open space is more difficult to photograph, and get a feeling of, as you well know, than a small space. Slowly I realized what I was doing, although the picture first of all seems to have ordinary

---

* 'Pearblossom Highway', originally commissioned by *Vanity Fair*, then abandoned by them as being too 'difficult' and expensive to print (see pages 148/9).

Pearblossom Hwy, 11–18th April 1986
(second version)
(photographic collage)

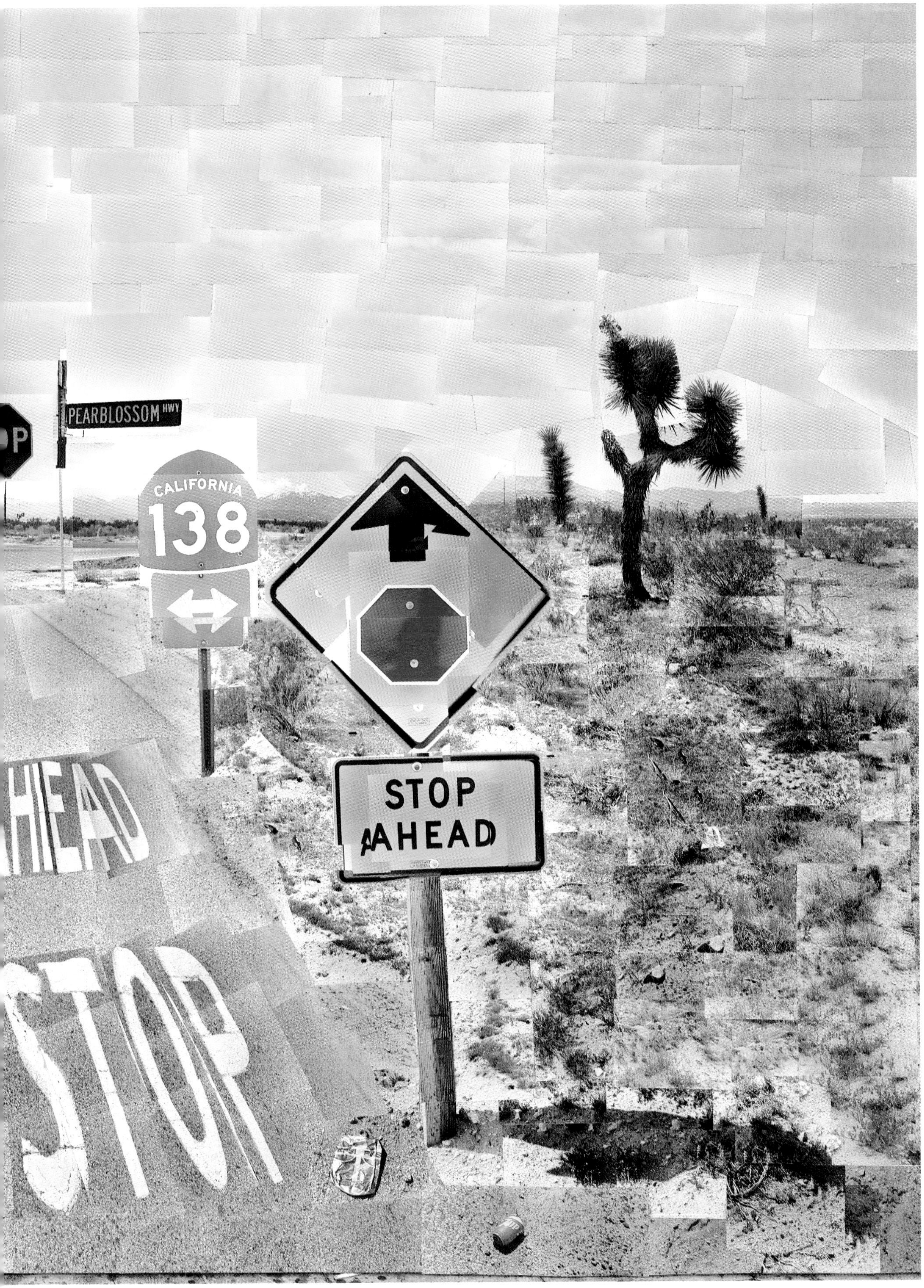
PEARBLOSSOM HWY
CALIFORNIA
138
STOP
AHEAD
STOP

perspective, in the sense that the space the picture describes seems totally believable. It only becomes a little strange when you start thinking about it or really looking at the image. Here is a picture of a wide open space that you can really experience, but at the same time you also feel close to everything, don't you? Close to the signs, close to the road, close to the shrubbery, close to everything – you can see the textures of things. You actually move to look at things. So the picture is dealing with memory in a different way from the previous pictures. First of all, three of us drove out to Death Valley and back, taking some photographs on the way – not many, but we had the experience of driving out into the space. We got to Furnace Creek, supposedly one of the hottest places in the Western Hemisphere, where it rains once every four years. The day we were there it rained!

Then I remembered there was a crossroads we had passed, which I thought could be more interesting. That picture was not just about a crossroads, but about us driving around. I'd had three days of driving and being the passenger. The driver and the passenger see the road in different ways. When you drive you read all the road signs, but when you're the passenger, you don't, you can decide to look where you want. And the picture dealt with that: on the right-hand side of the road it's as if you're the driver, reading traffic signs to tell you what to do and so on, and on the left-hand side it's as if you're a passenger going along the road more slowly, looking all around. So the picture is about driving without the car being in it. The more you look at it, the more you realize it's about *driving*.

It took us a week to make this, me, David and Charlie. We did the motel rooms at the same time but they're much simpler. I do think this kind of picture is getting more and

more *painterly*, which is very interesting. I'd started using a ladder on a previous picture – one I made in Pembroke Studios at Christmas over a period of about three weeks. I realized that you do get distortions in photographing a room, a kind of fish-eye effect, because you have to point the camera upwards. So I started using a ladder so that at least I could point the camera just *onwards*. In the landscape we needed a ladder even to photograph the small signs. If you stood on the ground, and included the edges of the signs in the picture, only the sky would show behind them. But, in fact, two of the signs are completely surrounded by the land. The picture was very complex to make. For instance, the lettering in the roadway was done about eight times, with eight different sets of letters to try to get the right angle, the way it *should* look.

PJ: When you work on a complex piece like that, it sounds as if it might develop an organic life of its own, and so turn out to be completely different from what you had anticipated. Would you then go back and rephotograph?

DH: Of course, there's no one viewpoint and so I can move things about if I want to. I can bring a tree in closer and things like that. The actual space, from one side to the other, is about five hundred yards, which is a considerable distance. If you stood near the yellow sign and just took an ordinary photograph you wouldn't see the other two signs. Maybe I should take you up there, it's about an hour away. Having seen the picture it would interest you to see the subject.

PJ: We should take some conventional photographs of Pearblossom Highway to contrast with what you've done. It's clear here that just as the individual images frequently overlap each other, so this reflects your own layering of time. Do you think an unsophisticated audience would appreciate this, perhaps even subconsciously?

DH: Yes, I think they would, without understanding how it was done. Obviously only people who are interested in constructing pictures are interested in the technique. Any viewer looking at the picture *knows* first of all, I assume, that the picture is intense, that there's a lot to look at. We chose deliberately a classical, American subject – a desert crossroad

photographed many times. The viewer is forced to wander around in the picture because I was literally wandering around the area. When you first look at it, it almost could be a conventional picture. It's only after half a minute that you realize it can't be and that keeps you moving in. I love the wide open spaces. I think they are good for the spirit. I love the feeling of taking a little walk in the wide open desert. The sky is massive and gives you a wonderful feeling. Somehow you feel the earth stretching for miles, without a vertical going up. You're aware there that you are on top of the earth – of course you are anywhere else, but somehow there you are more conscious of it. So all of this was put into the picture.

PJ: I think the picture is about twenty-five years of driving across America. You've put the past and the present into it. But one thing I notice, almost in the centre of the piece, is a single, one-point perspective image. Perhaps you feel there is still room for a traditional viewpoint occasionally?

DH: In fact, right in the middle is a single photograph that is hardly covered up. You see the whole thing – a totally conventional road disappearing into the distance.

David Hockney Photographing Pearblossom Highway, photograph by Paul Joyce

PJ: The picture which, in fact, anyone else might have shot as their one remembrance of the place for their album.

DH: Yes. It's also saying that you don't just dump one-point perspective, but that it is merely a part of a more complex perspective, which we must move on to. Greater complexity is a natural progression. One-point perspective is only a half truth, we *must* realize that . . .

PJ: It's interesting that the AHEAD and STOP signs on the road, although fractured by images in a very complex way, actually read quite clearly. Not so long ago, you would have surely made a more graphic, less 'traditional', rendering of lettering.

DH: Those signs must have been done about ten different ways. What's happening is that you read both the signs written on the road and the actual road signs, and when you see the words on the road you know they are under your feet. You're therefore actually looking down. By the time you get to the crushed Pepsi can it's as if you have turned your head! Yet it all looks right, doesn't it?

PJ: Yes. It's an extraordinary picture in that when you confront it for the first time, it seems like a familiar view. The viewer is immediately engaged. Then one realizes that you, the artist, have actually looked *everywhere* and that each look of yours is somehow reflected in at least one of hundreds of images. Surely this is the most complicated of your photographic pieces?

DH: By far, yes. It took us one week of going there to photograph *every* single day, then about another five days back here at the studio. Hundreds and hundreds of pictures were rejected because they didn't make the piece look right.

PJ: Do you think it's always necessary to have something which, graphically, will strike people as being familiar, in terms of the photographic work? Or do you think it's possible to smash that barrier of apparent realism?

DH: Yes, it is, I think it's possible to smash the barrier. I'm approaching it somehow, but exactly how I'm not sure.

PJ: One difference about this new work, compared to earlier photographic pieces, particularly the Polaroid work, is that when you started to do the Polaroids you would have thought three or four hours taking the picture was an immense time.

DH: Yes, I did, that is a difference. I think the longest time spent on the Polaroids was about five hours.

PJ: And now, in five hours, you're just beginning to look.

DH: Yes, I wouldn't think that was much at all.

PJ: You have come to the point when you can say time can be built into these pieces. And once that is accepted and dealt with, that time can be as long as you want – it could stretch to months or years. You might work on a painting for three years or longer and come back to it again and again. Would that not be possible with a photographic piece?

DH: It might be now. It's certainly going that way.

PJ: Your photographic work is moving much more towards painting now. You started by saying it's like drawing. I think it's become more like painting. Certainly in terms of your later paintings and collages, there are amazing points of similarity.

DH: Yes, it is all coming together – painting, photography, prints, everything. You can see the links clearly now. The paintings are becoming collage, the prints are becoming collage, even the prints that I did at Ken Tyler's* were actually collage.

PJ: Has the period of four or five years of occasionally very intense work on photographic pieces been necessary for a further advance in your other work?

DH: Yes, I do think so.

PJ: It comes back to that point of actually smashing through a barrier, doesn't it? You've actually got to break that apparently realistic surface and I think it is an aggressive act. One

---

* Ken Tyler, master printer, of Tyler Graphics, Inc. Publisher of *Paper Pools* and many recent lithographs by Hockney.

has to smash it. It's too powerful to be dealt with in any other way.

DH: Collage is the key to the escape from the old way of seeing. There's something deep and very profound about the idea of collage, something very true. Collage acknowledges surface and makes your eye realize that not only is there a change of surface, there's a change of many other things, when one thing is glued on to another on a flat plane. What is lack of space, for instance? Its opposite cannot be empty space, its opposite is a theoretical flat surface. You can only have a flat surface, a two-dimensional plane, in theory actually. Collage makes space by acknowledging this two-dimensional plane and gets closer to our experience of reality. It's like the verse:

> A man that looks on glasse,
> On it may stay his eye;
> Or if he pleaseth, through it passe,
> And then the heav'n espie.

George Herbert, *The Elixir*

The idea here of levels of seeing, the eye deciding where to go, is happening in those Xeroxes, isn't it? Glass is the theoretical flat surface, heaven is space. I first read those lines when I was about ten years old and they fascinated me. It describes how your eye can look on a surface or it can choose to ignore it and pass right through. The eye moves in space and it's that awareness that *makes* space for us. You begin to realize how foolish we've been to remain locked in the Western idea that the world goes on *without* us. I think this is deeply wrong. We are making *this* earth our consciousness, that is what I'm very aware of now. We could never prove it existed without us. When you get down to particle physics there's nothing there but energy. It all comes back to *us* – our minds, our heads, how we link with our own bodies and how that links with the world. I think there are vast changes coming. Do you remember *The Aquarian Conspiracy*? I liked the idea of that book and feel part of it myself, the growing awareness that you only change the world by changing yourself. A revolution in

A Diver, 1978
(coloured and pressed paper pulp
from the *Paper Pools* series)

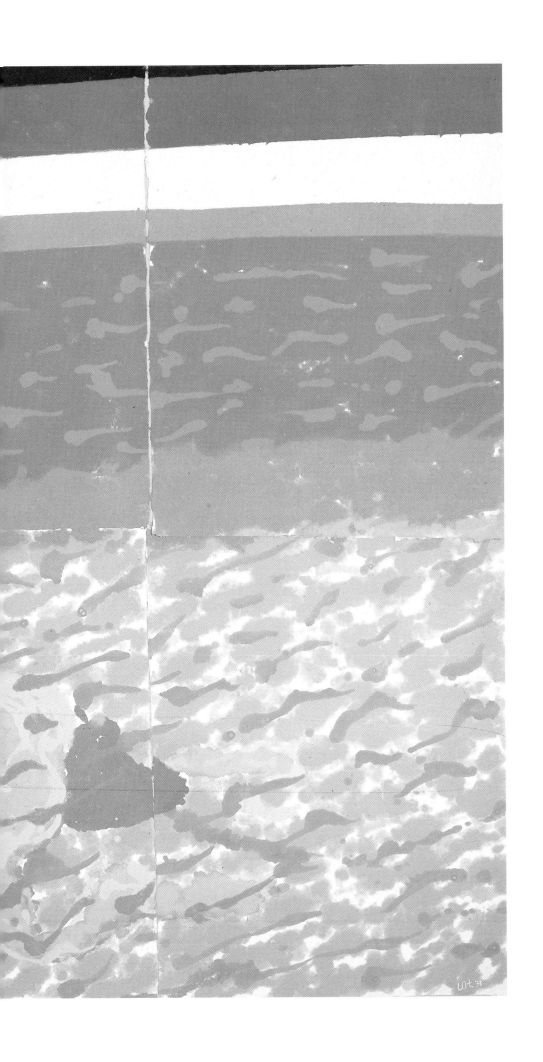

thought can be brought about by a change of awareness in us personally. It's very, very exciting, and it's way beyond those Marxist ideas of the way change would come. After all, those changes can never leave the material world.

PJ: I've had the feeling sometimes that there are parallel universes just a step away from us.

DH: Oh yes, they are here. There could be another Paul Joyce here doing something else. Do you remember, in Mexico City, I said that I felt there was far more *here*, right here? And only after that I began to read the theories physicists have come up with about alternative universes in the same place. Fascinating! And it all seems far more likely to me than planets with other people in, way out there. That belongs to the old idea of moving and journeying to find other living things.

PJ: Tell me about the Principle of Uncertainty that you mentioned earlier.

DH: The Principle of Uncertainty has philosophical implications; it deals with notions of measurement, and the fact that everything *isn't* measurable, which goes against prevailing Western ideas. After all, we can't measure anything without being aware that we are making the measurement. *We* are there. This makes it clear that there is no neutral viewpoint. It was Heisenberg who made this discovery in 1927. He'd gone to the Island of Helgoländ – a rather misty place in the North Sea – for a rest because they told him he'd been overworking. He took walks, as physicists do, to think. And he thought out this mathematical formula about measurement: that you cannot measure both the position and momentum of a particle. The theory isn't about error but about the fact that it's just not possible. The implications are vast and, of course, one of them is that there is no neutral viewpoint. And that leads on to relate consciousness to reality – consciousness cannot be separate from it. I understand this passion for walking – when you walk alone you think, don't you? You go off in your head and think about all kinds of things. I used to walk across the moors in Yorkshire, always alone, and I've learnt since that all theoretical physicists do that.

PJ: Can you talk about the idea you mentioned before – how in Western art one-point perspective led us to Leonardo da Vinci's war machines and ultimately to the cruise missile, whereas Eastern perspective led the Orientals not just to a different way of perceiving the world but to putting the invention of gunpowder simply to the making of fireworks.

DH: I said that we can't measure the world without knowing that it's us making the measurement, but also we can't make an H-bomb without the Principle of Uncertainty. We've got the H-bomb, it won't go away, but we've only taken one aspect of that principle and that has led us towards the bomb. If we took other aspects it might be fascinating.

PJ: There's something eloquent and intellectually appealing about the fact that a cruise missile locks on to a target through a computer representation of a photographic image of the vanishing point!

DH: Yes, but isn't there also a link between the perspective picture, which excludes you from its space, and the cruise missile, which would ultimately exclude us from the world? Only artists really go into this area – you have to be interested in attempts to construct representations of reality. Even the scientist, who is making a constructed picture of reality, doesn't link these ideas with the problems of the picture. We know that the picture has a powerful effect on us – it makes us see the world in certain ways.

PJ: Leonardo was working from a one-point perspective viewpoint but he was also dabbling in war machines and ways of approaching targets with his submarines and guns. There is an element of attack in the one-point perspective idea because you actually have to aim at a target, which might not exist in a particular picture, but logically those lines can be brought to bear on anything you want. And it's a very easy step from that to a projectile which is going to obey the same rules. What can we do about that?

DH: Well, changes happen slowly, as you know, even though we think the world's speeded up. I think the idea that people have understood, say, something that happened fifty years ago, absorbed it and now gone beyond it, is not possible. It often takes a great deal of time to *really* understand what the implications are.

PJ: What's the implication for the artist now?

DH: Well, you've heard people say: we've got too many images, we're saturated with images. In one way it's true, and in another it's not. There are thousands and millions of images, but not very many are memorable. Most will just disappear. If we are to change our world view, images have to change. The artist now has a very important job to do. He's not a little peripheral figure entertaining rich people, he's

really needed. When I realized that, it really thrilled *me*, because it means there's a purpose to what I'm doing. This is the reason why I've never bothered too much about the price of my work. I always thought it sad that it became so expensive, but you don't have to *own* the works for them to have an effect. It's not a matter of who owns them. I couldn't care less. It's research, my research, which ultimately can make a contribution to our awareness. In the end, art must reach everybody in some way. I loathe the notion of art just being for a few people.

PJ: Do you think that photography in some way mimics a pattern that the brain may have in recalling things? When we

Drawing for a Giant Crossbow by Leonardo da Vinci

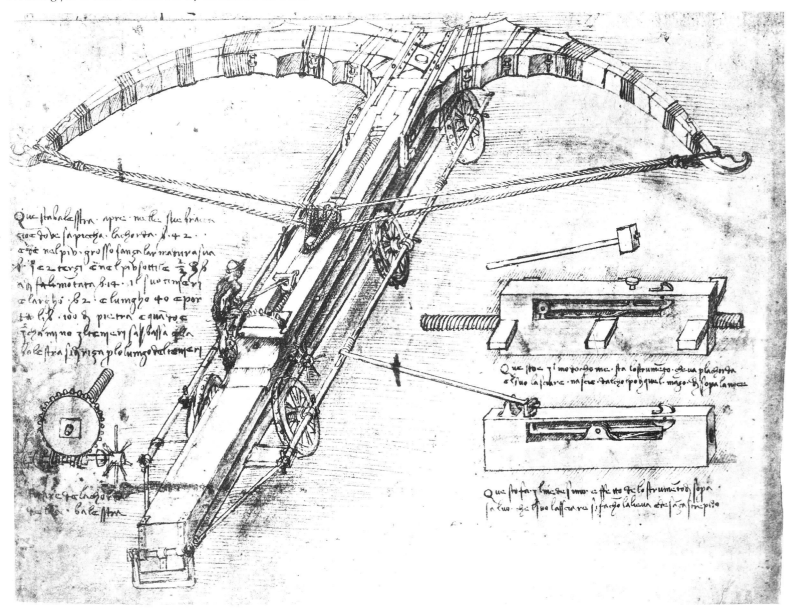

Interior, Pembroke Studios,
London, 1986
(photographic collage)

remember things – people, moments in our life – we have a tendency to stop time in our heads. Is this because we are used to looking at photographs, so the brain has, so to speak, assimilated the one-point perspective? Is there something actually built into the way we remember the world which seems to be photographic?

DH: I've always thought that Proust was very right. For instance, I was working on *Parade* and I went for a weekend to Connecticut to stay with one of the technical directors of the Metropolitan Opera. We went blackberrying. Now, as a child I used to go blackberrying on a railway embankment with my mother and brothers; we took cornflake boxes to fill with them. The sight of the blackberry bushes did not bring it back vividly, just a suggestion perhaps. But the moment I picked one and put it in my mouth, as it burst on my tongue, an incredibly vivid memory came back. It was so vivid that it was as if that time became *now*. It was also Proust's story, a non-intellectual experience that happens. You can't control the juices of the blackberry, or the madeleine. Something happens in your mouth and triggers something else which becomes incredibly vivid. It's of the past, but you're aware it's now.

I didn't get a great deal out of Proust at first, but there were things which absolutely fascinated me, particularly about memory. I have thought about the question: what is the memory actually like visually? Is it blurred, is it vague? You are aware of a kind of long-ago murky memory that you assume you could bring back, just as you are aware that you have to forget to be able to remember. Have you come across any books by Rupert Sheldrake? People have been looking in the brain for the memory, but they can't really quite find it as a physical part. But Sheldrake has this theory that there are fields which are outside our physical bodies, waves the memory can tune into. He opens up the possibility that there might be collective memories, which can be picked up. Some people suggested his theories were terrible bunk, but they do click a bit with me, and I'm not a scientific person.

Am I wandering off now? Well, I realize you want me to talk about the photograph. The thing is, I'm going on about memory because I've been trying to deal with it in these photographs.

Ultimately I think ordinary photography has made the world dull. There's *always* something everywhere, and it's always interesting. *You* make it interesting, even if it's not interesting in itself.

PJ: Your new Xerox pieces, the 'Home Made Prints', do seem to me to be an absolutely logical progression from your later, complex photographic work.

DH: Well, I realized that the crossroads picture is about many things, but it is also about a space. But I didn't photograph the space as a subject in any single picture there, other than the sole one-point perspective image in the middle. I was photographing surfaces, the road, the sign, a tree. It's all about surfaces. I then constructed it to give a feeling of space and you can rearrange the pictures. There's some fascination, some connection between space and a flat surface. I'd always been fascinated by space, and a theoretical flat plane. That's why I make pictures. It's putting something on a plane and in collage, two or three planes, more if you want.

A two-dimensional surface is incredibly fascinating because you can put more and more dimensions into it. It has always fascinated me and it must be the same with anyone who makes pictures. I've noticed this is true in movies, certainly the ones I react to and watch over and over again. Jacques Tati made marvellous use of the screen as a surface to show you space. You make the space in your head from his suggestions on a flat surface. That is much more thrilling than any attempts there have been at 3D, which are silly. You have to acknowledge the flat surface, and the single photograph has a great problem here, because your eye glides completely over it. It can't deal with its own surface. On a television screen showing a photograph of something, your eye goes clean through it as if it's a window. I'm beginning to realize there is something very dangerous about this.

PJ: I saw you put together a complete Xerox work from scratch yesterday, constituting six separate sheets. All the time you were reworking each individual sheet, sometimes five or six times, adding, subtracting. I can't think of any other printing process which would allow you to do that so fast and with such flexibility.

DH: The machine does what you want it to. And I've discovered that it can do far more than I thought. But the thinking process is similar to that involved with the photographic work.

PJ: As soon as you put two photographs together, in the way that you are now putting two Xerox copies together, something has changed irrevocably, hasn't it? The machine is no longer seeing. You are fooling the machine.

DH: This little machine, the camera, has been used for a hundred odd years in a very simple way. We just plunk it down, thinking that the camera sees what's in front of it. Well, it doesn't, actually. The most important thing that we feel and see – space – the camera cannot even record. But it is good for recording surfaces, and we can do something with that facility. I suspect laser printers are going to make the Xeroxes look like old etching presses. Lasers could totally revolutionize the printing of magazines. After all, the half-tone process which enabled them to print pictures on newspapers only began about 1910 and only flourished after the First World War. With the new Xerox work I'm *drawing*. If you just Xerox a photograph it's not going to look like this.

Everything seems to be coming together now. I sensed it before but I couldn't articulate it. I don't know where the journey will take me, but it's very exciting. I plod along, I'm a bit of a plodder. But each step leads me somewhere else.

Los Angeles:
March 1987

During the winter of 1986 and the spring of 1987 I kept in touch with David by phone. Although both our schedules were very crowded, we arranged to meet in Los Angeles during the last week of March.

By now I was used to finding organized chaos within the Hockney home. When I arrived David was sitting in a small lightproof tent in a corner of his vast studio with a scale model of his sets for Tristan und Isolde, *frantically fiddling with a miniature lighting rig. Jonathan Miller (the opera's director) and the conductor, Zubin Mehta, were due in the next day, and David had been working on the models for five months. Once again the tape machine was set aside. Hockney, Miller and Mehta retired into the tent for hours on end, and cigarette smoke billowed through the cracks and settled along the studio floor, reminding me of a Hollywood 'haunted house' set.*

In a couple of days comparative peace returned. By now David was physically and mentally very tired. The completion of the first editions of Home Made Prints clearly marked the end of his five-year preoccupation with the photograph. Now he was committed to a major retrospective exhibition (in February 1988 at the Los Angeles County Museum) and he had begun to paint again, much to the relief of countless gallery owners. Also, the arrival of Stanley (David's pet dog) had given him an inseparable companion and a new subject for his pencils and brushes.

David's return to painting also marked the end of our conversations. When the end came, as is usual with most endings, it came unexpectedly, although his final comment was what I had been seeking. The text is finished, and moves out of our hands. For the time being there is nothing more to say.

PJ: Do you think you could have undertaken the Home

Made Xerox Prints without having done the photographic pieces first?

DH: The Home Made Prints came out of work I did with Ken Tyler: I worked there for a year and a half, and all that work came out of the photography. But it was also the photography which drew me to the Xerox machine, because I realized it was itself a camera – one which confines itself to flat surfaces. The Xerox work is collage as well, and I think collage is one of the most profound inventions of the twentieth century in any way it's used. Although there's a playful aspect to collage, there's also a manipulative aspect, and it's usually used for manipulative purposes. However, cubist ideas can save us from being manipulated, because in cubism collage is seen to be collage.

One of the faults in the *Cameraworks* book is that the actual surface of the photographs is not shown. They were rephotographed in a conventional way, but at the time it didn't occur to me that the rephotographing of them should

At Home with David and Stanley,
photograph by Paul Joyce, May 1988

Act I of *Tristan und Isolde*, Los Angeles Music Center Opera,
December 1987 (sets and costume designs by David Hockney)

dwell not upon the image but upon the surface. The image, after all, can take care of itself. The photographer, as it were, walked through the surface and not upon it. It would have been better if the corners of the photographs had curled up, or something, just so that you were aware of the surface. Perhaps there should have been shadows from the lumps of the Polaroid prints themselves. We should be able to feel that grid much more, and not simply have white spaces there. Shadows would have helped the eye to sense an eighth of an inch of depth, which could be very strong in a flat photograph. It could look almost real. I played with this idea on the next-to-last page of *Vogue* with the object upon the page.

Surface is important in our way of seeing. We are aware of it and every mark made on it. Why should you cover up marks in painting? In Western painting it's very common to cover up marks, but it's not in Chinese painting. However, in Western drawing the covering up of marks is not considered to be a sign of competence. There are a few reasons for covering up a mark in painting: perhaps you just didn't like the mark and want to eradicate it to put another mark there. Perhaps you wished to give the effect of volume to an object,

and you used chiaroscuro, blending the shadows by using cross-hatching with a brush. Inevitably, some marks would get covered up in order to gain what you think is a feeling of solidity. People have failed to see that in very late Picasso this technique does not happen. He doesn't cover up his marks, and his work is more like Chinese painting for this reason.

If the marks are not covered, significant things begin to happen. In the oil painting of Ian, I've covered up marks to make volume, but in the others I haven't, and if I've tried to make volume I've done it in a stylistic way. The painting of Ian was done three years ago. I wouldn't paint it like that now. In the painting of Stanley [the dog] you can see all the marks, and you do in the Xeroxes. Nothing is covered up, and for some reason these pictures work well from a distance.

PJ: The marks are actually more significant from a distance.

DH: Yes, you don't feel as if you've walked away from me, do you? The painting of Ian stays over there on that wall, but these later still lifes don't. You feel as if you are right next to them, and the same happens with the picture of Stanley.

PJ: One of the first things you said to me about photography

Ian Watching Television, 1987
(oil on canvas)

was how good it was for representing flat surfaces. But when you're making the joiners and the photo-collage work, you're not actually dealing with flat surfaces. The very nature of the collage means that it's not flat.

DH: Well, there's no such thing as a flat surface: it's only a theory. A flat surface must be about measurement, about scale. If you really do get down to the surface of a piece of paper, you find it's full of bumps. So where are the flat surfaces? Are they just on the edges of bumps? The flat surface is a theoretical thing, and that's why it's fascinating. Any painter is fascinated by the flat surface.

PJ: Well, as soon as the painter begins to paint, it ceases to be a flat surface, anyway. Surely, a photograph, a photographic print, is probably the closest, artistically, that you can get to a flat surface?

DH: Yes, it is, because it's all seen at once, and therefore your eye takes in the whole of the surface instantly. But in the collage the eye can't do that, because collage entails another time existing there. When people make deceitful collage, Stalinist collage, they try to make it look as if it's all the same time. But honest collage is deliberately putting another time there, so that the eye will sense two different times, and therefore space.

In order to make a photograph like this, the photographer has to acknowledge his own presence: he is a participator in the events he portrays. Is Cartier-Bresson a participator in the events of the photograph we talked so much about?

PJ: In 'The Informer' he doesn't participate in what's happening, but his commentary is surely deeply concerned with the event. If he had not been there, we wouldn't know about it, would we?

DH: We could read about it.

PJ: Not that particular event. We may have read about countless events like that, perhaps, but they haven't stayed in our minds.

DH: Do you know that I saw Cartier-Bresson at work on a

Paris street? I didn't realize it was him at the time, but I thought: that guy seems to know what he's doing. By an incredible coincidence the very next day I met him in Claude Bernard's gallery. He had taken a drawing to them. I was impressed by the way he seemed to glide down streets, standing in corners so that he wasn't noticed. I saw him, but I'm quite observant.

It reminded me of the problem with the fly-on-the-wall documentary. The other day on a newsreel here they were talking about Los Angeles street gangs, and they showed you a prison which contained a lot of gang members. There the prisoners were, banging on the cell bars, so that at first I thought they were an unruly lot. I then realized it was the camera which was making them react that way, and the moment the camera passed by they probably went back to sleep. But the average viewer, who doesn't consider how pictures are made, must have thought that these prisoners were banging on their cells twelve hours a day. It's the same in other situations: when they see a camera in Northern Ireland they'll throw the bombs, or react in some extreme way. It's done because of the presence of the camera, and yet they still want you to think the camera wasn't there.

PJ: But when you shoot photographs, there's never any attempt at concealment. In fact, it's completely the opposite: there has to be an absolute collaboration between the subject and you.

DH: Yes. At one time I put my feet in the picture, and then I realized I couldn't do that because I was walking about too much. It does have to be a collaboration. I couldn't photograph the little girl on fire in Vietnam, because the subject wouldn't have been the girl so much as my cruelty. Why on earth didn't the photographer throw the camera away and help the girl, that's what we should ask. But there's a point about the documentary photograph: if the camera is there, it must be a participator, but if it pretends not to be, then there's deceit.

I've gradually become aware that two very important surfaces, continuously in front of us – the pages of the media, especially the pictorial pages, and the television screen itself

Self-Portrait, July 1986
(two panels) (Home Made Xerox print(s))

(one paper and one glass surface) – ask us to forget them, to look through them. The television picture is behind the surface – it's a box; and the photograph printed on the page is below the surface, so that you're not aware of the paper.

I did a piece for the Bradford *Telegraph & Argus* recently, and they rang up to say how thrilled they were. They said: it seems to pop off the page! I told them it had probably just popped on to the surface of the piece of paper, so that they became aware of looking at the paper, whereas they were not aware of looking at the other parts. That's the difference. If you're aware of looking, then you make the space.

PJ: But you also said there might have been a sense that work existed beneath the surface.

DH: I think we are aware of the surface of the paper because we're playing with it all the time, even with the surface of the photographs – leaving the rough edges.

PJ: One thing that strikes me about the Xerox work, however skilful and complex the procedure, is simply the very flat surface. It's the colour which makes the surface come alive.

DH: Of course, painters know about surface: only if you acknowledge surface can you go through it. We're aware of surface, for instance, on the cover of *Vogue*.

PJ: Very much so. You see the surface of the canvas, and the surface of the paint as well. What was the experience of doing this series of Xeroxes so intensely? I saw you only when you were starting them.

DH: I was very thrilled to find a totally new medium, which nobody had explored. I was interested in the Xerox more as a printing machine, whereas most people who had played with it before had only used the reproductive aspects, and had assumed the printing wasn't too good. But there is no such thing as a bad printing machine. If the machine works and prints, whatever qualities it has can be used. It must have some good qualities so long as it actually works.

PJ: But beyond the actual printing, or indeed before and during the printing, you're making choices all the time about what goes on to that machine, not only what the content is but what the colour is, and so on.

There is an element of the provocative about the Home Made Prints, quite apart from their content and the investigation of the process. They are challenging the fine art establishment centrally.

DH: They do that, but they do challenge other things too. I have made the point, even with the black-and-white ones, that the machine can't copy its own layers. People do use the word 'copier' a great deal, don't they? I'm trying to point out that it isn't a copier, because there's no such thing as a copy, really. Everything is a translation of something else, no matter how it's done: it's a variation of time.

My work is never finished: it all leads on. The Xerox work led me to devise a way of doing those pages for the Bradford *Telegraph & Argus*. Now that seems to challenge a great deal; for the newspaper, instead of reproducing my art and therefore commenting on it, made the page the piece of art. The page couldn't comment. Isn't that taking away an aspect of the newspaper itself? For instance, not long ago some prints of mine were shown in London, at the Royal Academy, but I didn't send them in. Later, someone posted me a cutting from the *Observer* complaining about the high price of the prints. They probably thought I'd be upset by this: they know I've always thought the art world was too greedy. But I wasn't unduly upset because I'd already figured out, if only vaguely, just where the Xeroxes would lead. I'd begun to stir round in my mind the idea that somehow the page of the newspaper could have an original print on it, which, of course, would be very cheap. But the *Observer* haven't printed a piece on this very cheap print I made for the Bradford newspaper. If it did, the *Observer*'s readers might think: why can't we have one?

New technology is enabling mass production to change, so that it is no longer about the possibility of making millions of identical objects, but about the possibility of making each one an individual object. Of course, this is a very great change, and, somehow, it must relate to this work. The newspaper's idea that it can only comment on art, that it's outside it, neutral, is a false notion.

I made a little edition with the Xerox work, and since I do them myself the nature of the edition is quite small. I don't want to spend days and days making thousands of a similar kind, so I'd make a different one, and then a different one again. Sometimes I'd get thirty to the edition, but the most I made was sixty. I sold them at a certain price because of the relatively small number of prints.

What was more interesting for me was where it took me beyond the work itself. The Xeroxes disturbed the print world because of the fixed idea of the craftsman on one side and the artist on the other. With these machines, the artist has to be the craftsman because he's part of the process. In etching and lithography, for instance, you work with a craftsman who knows a little bit more than the artist technically, but with the Xeroxes you can't have someone who knows more than you about the machine because he'd get in the way: there is no room for him. But it disturbs a very small world – the world of the craftsman working with the artist – and it's fun to disturb things a little! However, if you take the implications further, then things are disturbed far more than you would ever have thought.

Although all this work has come out of the photography, my ideas have changed and so our conversations have changed, because I understood things more clearly as I went on. When the *Cameraworks* book was finished, for instance, I was only just emerging to the perspective problem, which took me a while to understand fully. Issues of perspective are more wide-ranging than art alone, for all pictorial notions revolve around perspective. Slowly, the political implications dawned on me, as well as others, which I had never dreamed of before.

The people who make computer machinery at the moment are delighted with the way it can alter the photograph, but they are just thinking of images. If you think out the implications of the fact that you can alter them so easily, then things become even more interesting because you are removing the authenticity about reality that the photograph has had for a hundred and fifty years. People lost all interest in the artist's hand. In fact, they came to think it was less truthful.

The irony is that the computer does need a hand to be involved in the making of pictures, and collage needs the hand as well.

The very first photographic experiments I made were on a collage principle. Collage has been around now for seventy odd years, but it took me a long time to realize how profound an invention it was. Yes, you can make pretty pictures with the Xerox, but I knew it could be much more than that. But I enjoy using pretty pictures to make something more profound, and the knowledge that these pictures have a subversive side is deeply appealing!

I keep seeing examples of illustrative art which try to deal with social problems, as though there aren't pictorial problems which have any effect. Of course, a great many people think that my art hasn't much to do with social problems. I think it does, even if I'm just making a picture of my own back yard, which happens to have a palm tree and a swimming pool in it!

I don't think this work is going to end here, but I do see why there might be strong opposition to it, for there's a lot of vested interest in the neutral viewpoint.

PJ: Where is this opposition going to come from?

DH: From what we call the media, which is not quite what we think it is. The media still, to a certain extent, believes in the neutral viewpoint, whereas science has had to break away from it, and when it does it makes incredible discoveries. Well, there could be discoveries in other fields too.

People tend to think television news needs zappy pictures, so we are shown Rome burning rather than Rome being built. But we are shown that because the way of seeing the world, and the mechanical instruments that we use, find it much easier to deal with Rome burning than with Rome being built. And, of course, Rome burns far more quickly than it is built. Destruction is always faster than creation; dramatic destruction, that is, we wouldn't notice slow destruction. It comes down again to a question of time.

Working out the implications of my experiments is a bit like working out the idea that if mathematics is consistent it cannot be complete. There's something fascinating about that

*A Bounce for Bradford,
February 24th, 1987* A David
Hockney 'original' printed and
distributed by the Bradford
Telegraph & Argus in a Special
Edition dated 3 March 1987

idea, but it's not easy to realize the implications. The idea of the unknowable, which science didn't deal with for two hundred and fifty years, is now being confronted, and it's a deeply interesting area, particularly for all kinds of artists. I think we're bound to see a great change in pictorial ideas because of this work, and I'm sure it will have a political effect, as well, because it's about images and how we respond to them.

PJ: It's intriguing that all the photographic experiments led directly to the Home Made Prints, which, in turn, led to the

page of a newspaper, the simplest and cheapest and most easily available form of communication that exists in our society. You said that the newspaper piece was technically quite complicated. What exactly was the technique?

DH: It couldn't be done without the Xerox machine. I took away some processes that technicians had been doing, and returned them to the artist. I did the colour separations myself, but normally I would just have done the picture, with whatever colours I chose, and then the technicians would have processed it. In the end, all they had to do in Bradford

was something very, very simple. They didn't even have to check their colours against anything, because I told them just to use their standard four colours. In fact, there would have been nothing to check their colours against, for the picture was the thing itself. I'd taken away layers that we thought, perhaps, couldn't be taken away, that had to do with the processes of reproduction.

I delved into the printing process because printing is deeply connected with our way of seeing. The very word 'printing' has a lot to do with photography, because the photograph has to be printed, even if it's on a small piece of paper, as opposed to a transparency or a slide. If it can't be printed, it can't be seen by anyone, and therefore it won't have any effect. I'm aware now that we can change things, so I'm looking at all this with an amused eye.

I suggested many months ago that the catalogue for the Los Angeles County Museum should contain some pages made by myself. At the time I was thinking of the *Vogue* pages which I did, but now that I know how to use the paper itself as a medium, the exhibition can end by moving into the catalogue itself. My pages will be different because they won't be a commentary on the exhibition, they will be part of it, and all the other parts of the show will arrive at that point. I don't know yet what I'm going to do, but my hunch of planning it is right. I've certainly now found a way to use printing, not as a reproductive medium, but as a creative one. I don't want different printing or a different kind of paper inserted. The pages should be printed by the same presses in exactly the same way, just like the page for the Bradford *Telegraph & Argus*.

Some of my photographic ideas are no good for advertising because, essentially, they are anti-materialistic, but the paradox is that the newspaper page is about material, about the very page it's on, as a physical thing. This is why the image is so strong on that page: you look at the page, not through it, therefore recognizing the very paper itself. I think, somehow, I've been heading for this for years. I've always been interested in reproduction and I know full well that if art is not reproduced or reproducible, then it's hardly known. For instance, I've seen more Picassos in books than I've seen in real life, partly because I've sat down and looked through the whole of Zervos* three times. It would be an almost impossible task to assemble all those paintings together in one place, and yet they do exist all together in that book on the printed page. It is black and white, there's virtually no colour, but it is in itself a unique document.

I don't think printing is a side-issue, I think it's an important one. I must admit that sometimes I go down little side-lanes that turn out to be culs-de-sac, but sometimes they provide an angle which I can branch out from. Printing is an area which not too many artists think about. Andy Warhol is an exception. I think he understood intuitively a lot about printing as a medium, and his printed work is not very different from his so-called art-work. All his work involves printing and it's all just as effective in a printed book, which isn't the case, with, say, Picasso or Rembrandt.

PJ: But your work is very different, because your range and skill are much more extensive than Warhol's.

DH: Yes, but I just follow my intuition, usually wherever it leads me, and I'm aware that my work is known a great deal through reproduction. It couldn't be seen by nearly as many people if there were only the originals. You'd be surprised how few artists seem to take notice of this. An awful lot of pictures are reproduced once, and then they disappear, sometimes for good: a great deal of art does just vanish. When the first book, *Hockney on Hockney*, was done, the one I did myself, it occurred to me that bits of it might survive now. I don't know how many copies they published, but the book is spread far and wide.

PJ: Forty-six thousand copies were sold in the UK alone!

DH: Were they? Well, it was sold all over the world, so it must be well spread around. If there's a nuclear war, then perhaps some form of my work will survive, just in the shape of that book, as Picasso's would survive if all there was left was a Zervos. Of course, the great art of the past will survive,

---

* Zervos, a comprehensive catalogue of twenty-three volumes reproducing all Picasso's work in black and white.

Nu couché, 4th April 1932
by Pablo Picasso

if only because it exists in so many books now; that is, if anything survives at all! We have to remember how much art has disappeared: art is a lot more ephemeral than we think. Rembrandt's work is still with us, but that's only three hundred years old, not that old, really. We just don't know what the situation will be in another thousand years. Nevertheless, versions of his work will exist in a permanent way.

I may have digressed there, but it is all to do with the camera. Printing and ways of seeing have a very, very strong connection. Unfortunately, the media doesn't sense that, and it's as though it has one subject it can't comment on, which is its own limitation. It can't quite deal with anything outside itself.

PJ: I suppose the logical conclusion of this is that you will end up sometime doing your own book.

DH: I'm actually thinking of that now. I'm thinking of making a book in the form of, say, that *Interview** magazine where I did the page, using so-called cheap printing which we tend to think is not beautiful.

The first books I did were hand-made books. *Six Fairy Tales of the Brothers Grimm*, for instance, was hand-printed, and therefore somewhat expensive, especially for a book. I think it sold for four hundred pounds: a lot of money, although, considering the way it was made and hand-printed, it cost more to make than most books would sell for, and most people who bought it knew that.

I'd like to make a book which isn't simply reproductions, which uses ordinary printing machinery so that it would be cheap to make a lot of copies. I see, as I look at that *Interview* page, how I could do it, and how bold it could be. I will find a subject and I'm sure I'll do this book within the next year. Already we are looking at printers, and I'm thinking of trial ideas for the four-colour process.

The Home Made Prints are the reason why I've lost interest in other things. For instance, there's somebody called Peter Webb who's writing a biography of me, but I have little interest in it. First of all, I don't think artists' lives tend to be that interesting outside their work, and most artists work an awful lot. It should be the work that tells you about the person, so Peter Webb would be better off interpreting my work in some way. Anyway, I let him do it: it's his book, not mine. Mine would be quite different. I don't care about it at all, and he knows I'm indifferent towards the project. I told him I was also indifferent to Jack Hazan making his film about me. It was his portrait, not mine. It was not a self-portrait, it's a portrait of me by Jack Hazan, and I'm just, as it were, a model … Whether I like it or not is hardly the point, but I realized that if I'd done a portrait of somebody, and they didn't like it, and I did, then fuck them!

The book of mine occurred to me quite some time ago, but only now do I know, at least technically, how to start it. In fact, I think I'll make it on newsprint. There are different qualities of newsprint, and I'll probably pick the better ones because they will last longer. I'll do it in different ways, different forms, but I do want a period of painting first.

PJ: How do you think about our book?

DH: I think it's your book, really, although I'll make a lot of suggestions to you: ultimately it's yours, you are the person responsible. When I write things down it's usually after a period of clearing my head. Each lecture I give comes after a period of thinking and clearing things out, which does make me see more clearly myself. But I will certainly make suggestions for the printing of this book, partly because I realize the *Cameraworks* book didn't work, and I didn't know why, at first. When you begin to realize why things may not be working, that makes them more interesting and becomes part of it.

PJ: From what you've said over the last couple of days, it seems that the book we're doing could have something about it which makes it always living, in a sense, and not like *Cameraworks*, a dead record of something fixed.

DH: Everything dates after a while, and then comes back. Dating is just a process of change. For instance, there's the wonderful *New Yorker* cartoon of the man looking at the art deco objects and saying: this is a movement we've got bored

---

* *Interview* magazine, December 1986 issue.

of twice. Very funny, I thought! But with really interesting things, one begins to see them differently, and then they can settle down to being always there. I've witnessed that with Picasso in the sixties – when people thought his work had dated, stuck somewhere earlier, while contemporary art had advanced somehow. Dating is about fashion, which does affect everything, but there comes a point at which some things transcend fashion whereas others fall by the wayside: ninety-nine per cent of it does; it has to, we couldn't deal with it otherwise.

I don't think the individual artist should worry too much about this, he simply has to go on with his research. And it is the artists who make people look at the past differently: in that sense it's artists who make art history, not art historians. We tend to forget that, and even the historians forget it after a while! The past is constantly being re-evaluated so that it's kept alive. Art is either alive now, or it doesn't really exist, no matter when it was done.

When we did *Parade* at the Met, which consisted of a ballet and two operas, a critic called Clive Barnes wrote a piece saying the ballet was dreadful and he didn't feel like commenting on the operas. He said it was as though we'd gummed little graffiti on to the tomb of Satie. When I saw Barnes, about six months later, I said: you know, artists don't have tombs; they are either alive, or if they're dead nobody would notice the tombs. I told him I thought the metaphor was wrong, and he just nodded! I suppose they have to write things very quickly, and instant opinions should be taken with a pinch of salt.

PJ: Do you see the three or four years of intense work on photographs continuing in any recognizable form?

DH: I don't know. Certainly the intensity of the discoveries has worn off, and I'm working more slowly now. For instance, my discoveries with the Xerox machine at first were very intensive, I worked very hard, and then I stopped for a bit. I might go back to the work and use it, but what you can never do is make the discovery again – that you can only do once. I realized that body of work had within it a subject that future work could not have: it had the joy of discovery, which, by its very nature, can't be repeated.

I would only go back to photography now if I felt ready to push it in another way. 'Pearblossom Highway' was a big advance on almost anything else. It was much more complex, and yet a simpler image, almost straightforward at first glance. An awful lot of people probably don't realize just how complex it is, but it doesn't matter. That piece took a long time – virtually two months, the sort of time I wouldn't commit now. I've just spent five months doing an opera set, so I want to paint for some time now.

I have noticed people using the joiner ideas in magazines sent from Europe. Most of them are not very good, but some are beginning to get somewhere. I'm sure the minute people started on the work, they realized how complex it was going to be. They think it's rather easy when they just look at my work.

I've noticed that older photographers tend to dismiss these ideas, or simply don't like them, while the younger ones seem more open to them. I suppose it's the same old story: we ought to expect that; it's the case with most new ideas. When Picasso and Braque experimented with cubism it was the young who were excited, not the old. Nevertheless, there's a marvellous story about Matisse being told by Renoir that he didn't care for Matisse's pictures. Renoir was probably being very honest, but he was very nice to Matisse. I'm sure cubism wouldn't have meant too much to Monet, either, and he didn't die till 1926. It was right outside Monet's area, and he would have thought they were just young Turks doing something mad.

I noticed the criticism from older people myself. They were saying things like: you can't make good photography with a one-hour Fotomat, certainly you can't make art photography. Now, even in the art world they wouldn't say things like that, they'd know better. Nobody in the art world would say you can't make art from a piece of old wood, or a bit of plastic, or some trashy material, because they know perfectly well that it can be done. It seems to be the craft side of photography which is speaking here. The craftsman, who is not an artist, wants a beautiful piece of marble, whereas the artist knows perfectly well that if there's nothing else he'll use the old bit of wood: he has to.

PJ: I remember looking back on our conversations, and one thing you said really fascinated me. You said your photographic work was both a critique of and a commentary on photography, as much as being the work in itself.

DH: It is, but as far as I'm concerned, it changed photography for me. I get more and more letters now from people, and they're mostly young, and some of them are very perceptive. They see the implications of the ideas.

The power of these joiners is that we know they are collages. Compare them with the photograph I showed you yesterday in which the view from the window and the furniture in the room had been altered by the computer, not the camera. That only works for the conventional, one-point perspective picture. Cubism can save us from this and, in fact, cubism made possible the idea of collage, of the superimposition of one time level on another, therefore making the surface anything but flat. Of course, with Stalinist collage the picture is flat because the natural surface is taken away and replaced by another one. In montage, which is a slightly different thing, particularly with the work of that German, John Heartfield,* there's no deceitful attempt to make it look flat: we know it is montage, and there's no Stalinism. Quite the opposite.

PJ: And it was a political bombshell. Heartfield was vilified and his work was suppressed.

DH: It was done at a time when very powerful forces were against him, but perhaps that made him do it. We might expect that reaction.

PJ: He did create truthful images through that technique, projecting what might happen in the future.

DH: There's another aspect here. It's difficult with photography to actually know what the present is like, because

---

* John Heartfield single-handedly took the art of photographic collage from the province of Edwardian aesthetes and transformed it into a social and political weapon which he wielded mercilessly against the forces of Fascism in Europe. Bertold Brecht called him 'one of the most important European artists'.

there are too many pictures taken. I made a suggestion to somebody at the International Centre for Photography in New York for an exhibition. I said I had noticed over the years that in the photography of the nude there had been a movement towards closeness, and that if you looked through all the magazines showing nudes, which have been produced for a number of years now, you could detect that movement, and make an interesting exhibition.

Of course, it ought to be the museum's job, to look at these developments in art and photography. But this proposed exhibition would entail using photographs by people we have never heard of. Maybe, within that world, particular photographers are well known. Certainly some are much better at depicting flesh than others are; that we can see. But they have got to the point where, with a single lens, they can't get any closer. If you got really close, you'd have to do a joiner like the one I did of Theresa Russell. That one was done, in a sense, as a commission, but I've often thought I should make one with a boy. I tend to like the bodies of boys, so it could be a turn-on; something more interesting for me, at any rate. But it would be about closeness first of all, which is totally impossible from any single viewpoint.

I've noticed there are always photographers being discovered from the past, and I suspect this will go on happening because there are far more photographs being made than there are paintings. Perhaps we'll discover painters as well, although they tend to be somewhat isolated people, working very quietly because that's their nature. Photographers tend to be the opposite. Museums which show photography usually go along with the current fashion, but, of course, fashion does change, and the moment it changes we rediscover something from the past which was overlooked in the previous fashion. It's a very natural process.

PJ: I'm inclined to think that kind of documentation is passing us by. I rather think the work you've done, and the way you've changed photography, means that it's never going to be the same again: it's not going to be as self-absorbed.

DH: What I've done proves that photography is part of pictorial invention. It can't be separate now, as it has been

The Mandolin
by Georges Braque, 1910

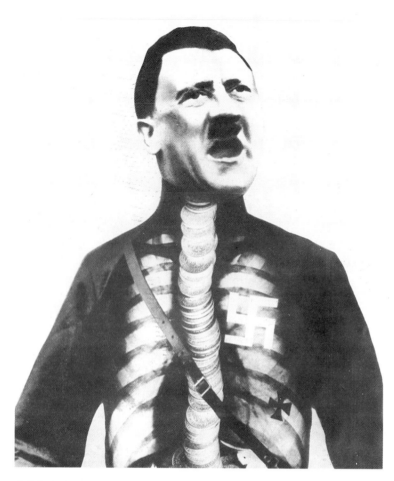

Adolph the Superman Swallows Gold and Spouts Junk,
photomontage by John Heartfield, 1932

treated for so many years. The idea, the very words 'photo-graphic realism', mean a very accurate perspective picture with everything in proportion, implying a certain kind of measurement. As far as I'm concerned, I've changed that, but whether I've changed it for others is hardly for me to say.

Many more people now go to photographic touring shows, and I've no doubt that's because they attract the photography world itself, which is enormous, and it's all practitioners. There are probably very few people like yourself, who are interested in theoretical aspects, and who also make pictures. There may be thinking people deeply interested in photo-

graphy, but there are huge numbers of people who simply take photographs, who are attempting to depict what they think reality is. The idea that the photograph is the ultimate depiction of reality is, of course, naive, if you really think about it; even if you think for only ten minutes! Never has pictorial form stood that still. But I've no doubt at all that at each period people thought they were dealing with reality.

I think we're living at a time when this problem about photography being seen as the ultimate depiction of reality is beginning to break down – partly through what I did myself, and partly because of the new technology, what the computer can do, and so on. We don't know what photography will look like in two hundred years or so, but I suspect it will look different, very different. This is the exciting thing: photo-graphy has been brought back into the area that painting has always dealt with.

PJ: So the camera could become a helpful piece of equipment rather than an objective, cold and calculating scientific instru-ment. The camera has got you closer to your subject, hasn't it?

DH: Yes, but I think all perspective photography has distance built into the picture.

PJ: Distance from the subject?

DH: A distancing effect, although many people thought the opposite. It only seems to bring us closer if you accept its spatial ideas. If you don't, then you see a distance, but I admit not many people see it that way.

PJ: If I'm not always up with you in our discussions, I do know enough for certain assumptions to be made between us about the work you've been doing. But when people who don't know how these pictures were put together start to read this text, it might be illuminating for them to have some idea of how you approach a particular picture. I suggest we take the example of the British Embassy joiner, which you did in Tokyo. For a start, which camera did you have in your pocket? Was it the small 110?

DH: No, I think it was the Nikon 35mm. I was on a visit to

Japan, mainly for the paper conference, but I was going to give a lecture about photography as well, and the British Embassy was organizing a translator for me. We had been invited to lunch there, Gregory [Evans] and Paul Cornwell-Jones and I. Just before lunch we were talking to the British Ambassador, who was obviously something of a scholar and spoke very good Japanese. We talked about pictures for a bit, particularly Japanese art and the Japanese way, or rather the Chinese way, of seeing. He was talking about perspective, and the different ways of depicting space in pictures, and I told him I had been experimenting with photography, and wanted to make a picture over lunch of the assembled company at the table. He said that was fine, and so I took the photographs over the period of the lunch. I tried to do it without intruding too much, so I never moved from my place at all.

When I put the picture together, it really did look as though the viewer was in my place at the table, having conversations with the other people. Each person has several heads, apart from the man sitting right next to me, and so it took quite a while to construct afterwards. I had the films processed in Tokyo, but just looked through them there: I didn't make the collage until I returned home. I remember it took quite a while because I had to use the curves. Later on I could have got rid of those curves if I'd wanted to, but I would have needed more photographs, and I couldn't very well go back and re-create that scene, as I could with some of the other joiners. At that time the photography, the actual taking of the pictures, had always been done in one go. Later on they began to spread over days and days as they got more complex. The taking of the British Embassy picture was probably spread over an hour, not a lot longer.

PJ: But it's clear you were watching all those people very carefully. Look at the way the Ambassador seems to have his arm wrapped around himself! Perhaps it's a little joke about the man, too.

DH: Yes, he seemed to be a very confident character, so I even had him putting his arm on his own shoulder!

PJ: Did you plan that as you took the pictures?

Luncheon at the British Embassy,
Tokyo, February 16th 1983
(detail) (photographic collage)

DH: I wasn't sure, no. I could have rearranged them another way. I just happened to arrange them in that particular way. In the show at the ICP there was a big picture of the Grand Canyon which was actually photographed in 1982. I laid only one down in 1982, and I thought it was interesting: then I re-collaged it this year, but I laid it down differently. I didn't curve it, and I thought it was much more interesting in the space.

Then I realized I could lay down a few others in different ways because of what I had learned. Meanwhile they got more complex. The first one to take more than a day's shooting was the 'Place Furstenberg', which was spread over four days. Later on 'Pearblossom Highway' took nine days of photography.

PJ: And you'd actually go back to the location with the beginnings of the collage?

DH: Yes, with 'Place Furstenberg' I did, otherwise I wouldn't have known how to take the other pictures. With that one, which I did for *Vogue* in Paris, I was staying in a hotel room near the *Vogue* offices, and I went first to the Place Furstenberg, took some pictures, got them processed, and started gluing them down. Then I took the piece back with me. I had to have it with me, otherwise I wouldn't have known what to do next. I took it back three times. With 'Pearblossom Highway' there was a small version and a larger one. The small one had to come first: every day we took it back in the van to the location. After that experience I thought the big one would be quite simple, but it took about a month to lay down.

PJ: And you changed the sky completely?

DH: Yes, I changed it two or three times. And each time I changed it, the cost of the processing was about three hundred and fifty dollars. That's the last one I've done, really. I haven't done anything since.

PJ: The joiners are getting more and more complex now. There's a larger commitment of time, and a further commitment of looking as well. Do you have a notion of future photographic work at all, or is it just a blank?

DH: It's a blank. But I know how to push the ideas further, how to make different spaces, only I want to take that into painting now. With painting, the picture can be much more vivid, and the space can be made to look believable. It has all come out of the photography, but I think I can give that up now, and leave it to other people. Perhaps someone else might develop these ideas.

There are two things about using the joiners in advertising: firstly, they are not easy to do, and the more complex the space, the more complex the picture becomes; secondly, they don't really work for advertising purposes because there's a side to the joiners that's anti-materialistic, that's more interested in the space than the objects in that space. I think that's true in these new theatre sets here. What thrills people looking at these is not the objects themselves, but the spatial feeling. They thrill me! The objects make it, but it is the space we are aware of more. In that sense they relate directly to the photography.

PJ: Do you feel the theatre designs would be different if you hadn't been through the photography?

DH: Oh yes. I don't think I could play the games with space that I'm playing here. Just like the photographs, the viewer is totally drawn into the space, no matter where you are in the theatre. It's not a box that begins over there, which you look into. You feel you are actually on the ship; in the castle garden; on a clifftop, don't you?

PJ: Very much. When you went into photography, did your instinct tell you that you would emerge richer from the experience?

DH: Yes, it did: within a very, very short period it told me that. These were discoveries. They may not have been new discoveries, but they were certainly profound discoveries for me with incredible implications, philosophical implications. These pictures are all spatial, and if they are spatial they must be complex. After all, spatial ideas take us to questions about our own identity. Where are we, and who are we?

These ideas affected the painting immediately: I realized there could be totally new spaces in paint. It's only painting which can make these, not photography. I felt I'd taken photography to a certain limit. Photographers here, talking about the 'Pearblossom' piece, said: it isn't photography, it's painting. I could dismiss that as just something photographers would say, so that their work might go on undisturbed, but it *is* photography, even if I am, as it were, putting drawing into it. After all, the only instrument I used was a camera, and the only colours and processing used were photographic. True, I could change the colours, and I did that with the 'Pearblossom' sky, but the medium remained photographic. The joiners do get close to painting because there is a different space made from the one the camera sees ordinarily. Once I'd got to 'Pearblossom Highway' I felt photography was finished off for me. I know I could go on making more complex pieces, interiors especially, but I'm not sure I'll bother now. I'd rather do things in a more immediate way, through painting.

PJ: We've spoken about the Xerox work, and I know you've done a lot of it, but it hasn't been shown.

DH: I have done a lot, but we just published thirty-two of those pieces. I didn't want to publish some of the first ones. Of course, this work took me a step further; it enabled me to do those two pieces for the newspapers – the *Interview* piece in New York and the Bradford piece. Printing in magazines or books is a much more interesting area to move into because the artist can use commercial printing now as a direct medium, and not as an aloof reproduction medium. This means one can make much more interesting books, even though they're printed very, very cheaply.

I liked the opportunity of doing the piece for *Interview*, and for the Bradford newspaper. That is not a reproduction of the print I've made: it is the print. The process is therefore more direct, and looks more direct. You feel that straight away. Anybody opening the newspaper can see it. This is a fascinating area to have come out of photography. Here is a camera which deals with flat surfaces, the reproducing camera, the non-spatial camera, which is a Xerox machine as well. This opens things up to artists in a way they've not thought about. Artists have much too eagerly accepted the reproducing qualities of printing and photography, which, in many ways, distance the work from us.

If you look at some of my work in the eighties, you'll see that a great deal of it is actually about printing. It begins with the little book I did for 'The Artist's Eye' in 1982, which is about printing, about reproduction. The exhibition was about looking at pictures in a room, and in the introduction I was critical of photography in some ways, but most of the criticisms I attempted to deal with a year or so later. Then the *Vogue* piece was about printing: it was not just reproductions of my work. It is the work, the piece itself. Then the Home Made Prints catalogue is about itself, as well, it makes references to itself. And the 'Faces' catalogue did that too. So all this work came out of the photography; and yet moved quite away from it. If you just happened to see one of those catalogues you wouldn't directly connect it with the photographic ideas, although, if you had looked around, and you were intelligent, you would quickly connect them.

In this sense, the photography has not ended; it goes on and on, but I'd much rather go back to working very directly, and that means painting on canvas. I would now like to paint, that's what I really want to do. That's my last word.

David Hockney
Chronology

Visits Egypt and Los Angeles, 1963. Makes series of etchings 'The Rake's Progress', 1963, and *Six Fairy Tales from the Brothers Grimm*, 1969. Designs sets and costumes for 'Ubu Roi' at the Royal Court Theatre, London, 1966. Travels to Japan, 1971. Film 'David Hockney's Diaries' made by Michael and Christian Blackwood, 1971. Lives in Paris, 1973–5. Designs sets for the ballets 'Septentrion', 1974, and 'Varii Capricci', 1983. Designs sets and costumes for operas, 'The Rake's Progress', 'The Magic Flute', 'Parade', 'Les Mamelles de Tiresias', 'L'Enfant et les Sortilèges', 'Le Sacre du Printemps', 'Le Rossignol', 'Oedipus Rex' and 'Paid on Both Sides', 1975–83. Film about Hockney, 'A Bigger Splash', made by Jack Hazan, 1974. Makes large scale lithographs, 1976. Makes etchings to illustrate *The Man with the Blue Guitar*, by Wallace Steven, 1977. Makes lithographs and series *Paper Pools*, made with paper pulp at Tyler Graphics, Bedford Village, New York, 1978. Travels to China, May–June 1981. Makes composite polaroid and photographic collages, 1982–4. Makes multi-colored lithographs at Tyler Graphics, Bedford Village, New York, 1984–5. Designs cover and forty pages for the December 1985 issue of French *Vogue* magazine. Makes Home Made Prints (color Xeroxes) at Los Angeles studio from February–October 1986. Publishes catalogue of *Home Made Prints*. Designs sets and costumes for 'Tristan und Isolde' for the L.A. Opera Company 1986–7. Designs catalogue to accompany drawing exhibition at Loyola Marymont University, Los Angeles, in 1986–7. Creates twenty-four original pages for his book, *David Hockney: A Retrospective*, 1987. Writes, directs and is featured in the film 'A Day on the Grand Canal with the Emperor of China or Surface Is Illusion But So Is Depth', produced by Philip Haas, 1987–8. Creates original prints for local, national and international publications in connection with his major Retrospective, 1988.

One-man Shows
1982–8

1982
André Emmerich Gallery, New York. Christie's Contemporary Art, New York. L.A. Louver, Venice, California. Centre Georges Pompidou, Paris. Knoedler/Kasmin Gallery, London. Rex Irwin Gallery, Sydney. Susan Gersh Gallery, Los Angeles. New York Public Library, New York.

1983
André Emmerich Gallery, New York. Knoedler/Emmerich Gallery, Zurich. Richard Gray Gallery, Chicago. L.A. Louver, Venice, California. Knoedler/Kasmin Gallery, London. Nishimura Gallery, Tokyo. Bjorn Bengtsson, Sweden. Walker Art Center, Minneapolis, Minnesota ('Hockney Paints the Stage'). Hayward Art Gallery, London. Thomas Babeor Gallery, La Jolla, California. William Beadleston, Inc. Fine Art, New York.

1984
Museo Tamayo, Mexico City ('Hockney Paints the Stage'). Photography Gallery, Milwaukee Art Museum. Art & Sport Gallery, Belgium (prints). Bjorn Wetterling Gallery, Stockholm (prints and drawings). Knoedler Gallery, Zurich (selected prints). Art Gallery of Ontario, Toronto ('Hockney Paints the Stage'). Museum of Contemporary Art, Chicago ('Hockney Paints the Stage'). Knoedler Gallery, Zurich (prints). André Emmerich Gallery, New York (new paintings and drawings). Jeffrey Fraenkel Gallery, San Francisco (photographic collages). Fort Worth Art Museum, Fort Worth, Texas ('Hockney Paints the Stage'). Greenberg Gallery, St Louis (photographic collages). Milton Keynes Library, England, April/May (from travelling Hayward Art Gallery Exhibition on photography). Richard Gray Gallery, Chicago (new drawings). Galerie Esperanze, Montreal (prints and photocollages). Carpenter/Hochman, Dallas (photographic collages).

1985
San Francisco Museum of Modern Art, San Francisco ('Hockney Paints the Stage'). Hayward Gallery, London ('Hockney Paints the Stage'). Greg Kucera Gallery, Seattle, Washington (prints and photocollages). André Emmerich Gallery, New York (photocollages). Knoedler Gallery, London (lithographs, paintings and collages). André Emmerich Gallery, New York (paintings from the 1960s). College Art Gallery, New Paltz, New York (photocollages). André Emmerich Gallery, New York (new lithographs and paintings). Nishimura Gallery, Tokyo (new lithographs). Richard Gray

Gallery, Chicago, Illinois (new lithographs). L.A. Louver, Venice, California (new lithographs). Galerie Claude Bernard, Paris (new lithos, photocollages, drawings and paintings). New York State University at Albany, Albany, New York (photocollages). College of Santa Fe, Santa Fe, New Mexico (photocollages). Fundacao Calouste Gulbenkian, Lisbon (travelling photography show). Museum of Art, Oporto (travelling photography show). Fundacio Caja de Pensiones, Madrid (travelling photography show). Fundacio Caja de Pensiones, Barcelona (travelling photography show). Recontre Internationales de la Photographie, Arles. (photocollages).

1986
Contemporary Art Center, Honolulu, Hawaii ('The Rake's Progress', theatre sets 'Bedlam' and 'Auction Scene', models, drawings and etchings). Honolulu Academy of Art, Honolulu, Hawaii (photocollages, painting and drawings). Art Center College of Design, Pasadena, California (photocollages, cibachromes, Polaroids and new lithographs). Harvard University, Cambridge, Mass. (lithographs). Tate Gallery, London (Tyler prints). Gallery One, Toronto (photocollages and theatre drawings). 'Photographs by David Hockney' (organised by the International Exhibitions Foundation, Washington, D.C.) travelling to the following institutions from April 1986–April 1989: Boca Raton Museum of Art, Boca Raton, Florida; Davenport Art Gallery, Davenport, Iowa; Helen Foresman Spencer Museum of Art, Lawrence, Kansas; Elvehjem Museum of Art, Madison, Wisconsin; The Santa Barbara Museum of Art, California; Toledo Museum of Art, Toledo, Ohio; John and Mary Ringling Museum of Art, Sarasota, Florida; Akron Art Museum, Akron, Ohio; Snite Museum of Art, Notre Dame, Illinois; Philbrook Art Center, Tulsa, Oklahoma; Winnipeg Art Gallery, Winnipeg, Manitoba; Jacksonville Art Museum, Jacksonville, Florida; Cheekwood, The Fine Arts Center, Nashville, Tennessee; Springfield Art Museum, Springfield, Missouri; De Cordova and Dana Museum and Park, Lincoln, Mass; Institute of Contemporary Art, Philadelphia, Pa; Joseph and Margaret Muscarelle Museum of Art, Williamstown, Va. Matrix/Berkeley, University Art Museum, Berkeley, California (paintings and photographic collages). André Emmerich Gallery, Zurich. (lithographs and one painting of 'The Mexican Hotel Courtyard'). International Center of Photography, New York (photocollages and composite Polaroids). Travels to: Museum of Art, Tel Aviv, Israel; and Polaroid Corporation, Boston, Mass. Kaj Forsblom Gallery, Helsinki (photocollages and lithographs). Art Museum of Santa Cruz County, California (lithographs). 'Photographs by David Hockney' (organized by the British Arts Council, London) travelling to: Museo di Storia della Fotografia Fratelli, Alinari, Florence. In Japan: Toyama Prefectural Museum of Art; Tokyo Departmental Store, Tokyo; Tochigi Prefectural Museum of Fine Arts; Fukuoka Municipal Museum of Art; Museum of Modern Art, Hyogo. In New Zealand: McDougall Art Gallery, Christchurch; Dunedin Public Art Gallery; Wellington City Art Gallery; Auckland City Art Gallery. L.A. Louver, Venice, California ('Home Made Prints'). André Emmerich Gallery, New York, N.Y. ('Home Made Prints'). Knoedler/Kasmin Gallery, London ('Home Made Prints'). Nishimura Gallery, Tokyo ('Home Made Prints').

1987
Erika Meyerovich Gallery, San Francisco, California (lithographs and photocollages). Loyola Marymont University, Laband Art Gallery, Los Angeles, California (portrait drawings from 1966–84). Marian Locks Gallery, Philadelphia, Pa. (lithographs). National Museum of Photography, Film and Television, Bradford, England ('Home Made Prints'). New Mexico State University Art Gallery, Las Cruces, New Mexico (photocollages and Polaroids). Visual Arts Museum, New York (drawings). Gallery One, Toronto (20 years of prints). Haggerty Museum of Art, Marquette University, Milwaukee, Wisconsin (drawings, photocollages and prints from the collection of Dr Stan Sehler).

1988
'David Hockney: A Retrospective', Los Angeles County Museum of Art, Los Angeles, California (paintings, drawings, prints, photography, and stage designs from 1954–1988). Travels to: The Metropolitan Museum of Art, New York; The Tate Gallery, London. Santa Monica College, Santa Monica, California (photocollages). Columbus Museum of Art, Columbus, Ohio (photocollages). André Emmerich Gallery, New York (drawings).

Group Exhibitions
1982–8

1982
'Group V', Waddington Galleries, London, January 7–30. 'Important Prints', Getler/Pal Gallery, New York, December 22, 1981–January 23, 1982. 'Instant Fotografie', Stedelijk Museum, Amsterdam, December 4, 1981–January 17, 1982. Group Show, Dorothy Rosenthal Gallery, Chicago, May. 'Fast', Alexander F. Milliken, Inc., New York, June 11–July 15. 'Domestic Relations', Newspace Gallery, Los Angeles, June 8–July 30. Group Show,

Petersburg Press, London. 'Faces and Figures', Galerie Beyeler, Basel. '1960–80: Attitudes/Concepts/Images', Stedelijk Museum, Amsterdam, April 9–July 11. 'Photographs By/Photographs In', Daniel Wolf, Inc., New York, September 14–November 13. 'American/European Paintings', L.A. Louver, California, August/September. 'Erotic Impulse', Roger Litz Gallery, New York, September 11–October 6. 'Representational European Painters and their Forerunners', Marlborough Gallery, New York, November 6–27. 'Faces Photographed: Contemporary Images', Grey Art Gallery, New York University, November 9–December 23. '1982 Carnegie International', Museum of Art, Carnegie Institute, Pittsburgh, Pennsylvania, October 23, 1982–January 2, 1983; Seattle Art Museum, Washington, February 10–March 27, 1983; Art Gallery of Western Australia, Perth, June–November 1983; National Gallery of Victoria, Melbourne; Art Gallery of New South Wales, Sydney. 'Paper as Image', Sunderland Arts Centre and touring Cambridge, Bangor, Nottingham, Southampton, Brighton and London, November 1982–March 1984.

1983

The Metropolitan Opera Centennial: 'A Photographic Album', International Center of Photography, New York, September 30–November 13 (travels). 'Brooklyn Bridge Centennial', Brooklyn Museum, New York, May–September. '10 California Photographs: In Color', Oakland Museum, Oakland, California, May–August. 'Personal Choice', Victoria and Albert Museum, London, May–September. 'Photography in Contemporary Art: the 1960s to the 1980s', National Museum of Modern Art, Tokyo, October 7–December 4 (travels). 'Photographic Visions', Los Angeles Center for Photographic Studies, Los Angeles, California, September 10–October 16. 'American/European Painting and Sculpture', L.A. Louver, Venice, California, November 11–December 10. 'Artists and the Theatre', Herbert Palmer Gallery, Los Angeles, February. 'Britain Salutes New York' (Caro, Hockney, Nicholson), André Emmerich Gallery, New York, April 27–May 27. 'Major Prints', Getler/Pall Gallery, New York, June–August. 'Acquisition Priorities: Aspects of Post-War Painting in Europe', Solomon R. Guggenheim Museum, New York, May 19–September 11. 'Group Exhibition', André Emmerich Gallery, New York, December 9–31. 'Painter as a Photographer', Camden Arts Centre, London, and travelling to Windsor Castle and the National Museum of Photography in Bradford, July–November.

1984

'Jim Dine and David Hockney: Works on Paper', Patricia Heesy Gallery, New York, May 8–June 3. 'Contemporary and Modern Drawings, Collages and Paintings on Paper', Jack Rutberg Fine Arts, Los Angeles, February 25–March 31. 'Face to Face', Institute of Contemporary Art, University of Pennsylvania, Pa., June 15–July 29 (photographic collages). 'Olympian Gestures', Los Angeles County Museum of Art, Los Angeles, June 7–October 7. 'British Painting', Knoedler/Kasmin Gallery, London, June 15–July 15. 'The Hard Won Image', Tate Gallery, London, July 4–September 9. 'Automobile and Culture', Museum of Contemporary Art, Los Angeles, July 21, 1984–January 6, 1985. 'Hockney Prints', Mira Godard Gallery, Toronto, June. 'Landscapes: 1884–1984', Ulrike Kantor Gallery, Los Angeles, July–September. 'American/European Painting, Drawing and Sculpture', L.A. Louver, Venice, California, July–September. 'Frederick R. Weisman Foundation Collection of Contemporary Art', Palm Springs Desert Museum, California, January 7–February 26, and travelling to the Albuquerque Museum, New Mexico, March 11–May 6; The San Francisco Academy of Art, July 17–August 17; Utah Museum of Fine Arts, Salt Lake City, September 16–November 11; The Oakland Museum, Oakland, California, January 1985–February 1985; Hara Museum, Tokyo, March 1985–May 1985; Israeli Museum, Jerusalem, September 1985–November 1985. 'Modern and Contemporary Masters', Richard Gray Gallery, Chicago, February 11–March 24. 'Master Drawings 1928–1984', Janie C. Lee Gallery, Houston, Texas, March–April. 'The Folding Image: Screens by Western Artists of the Nineteenth and Twentieth Centuries', National Gallery of Art, Washington, D.C., March 4–September 3; Yale University Art Gallery, New Haven, Ct., October 11, 1984–January 6, 1985. 'Drawings, 1974–1984', Hirshhorn Museum and Sculpture Garden, Washington, D.C., March 15–May 13. 'Artist in the Theatre', Hillwood Art Gallery, Long Island University. Greenvale, New York, March 16–April 12; Guild Hall Museum, East Hampton, New York, June 9–July 15. 'The Figure in Contemporary Art', Maier Museum of Art, Randolph Macon Women's College, Lynchburg, Va, March 18–April 15. 'Contemporary Issues', Holman Art Gallery, Trenton State College, Trenton, N.J. March 28–April 18. 'Twentieth Century Works of Art', Stephen Mazoii Gallery, New York, May 1–June 30. 'The Skowhegan Celebration Exhibition', Hirschl and Adler Galleries and Hirschl and Adler Modern, New York, May 1–31. 'Reading Drawings: A Selection from the Victoria and Albert Museum, London', The Drawing Center, New York, June–July 28. 'Swimming and Other Pools', Getler/Pall/Saper Gallery, New York, June 20–August 31. 'Gemini G.E.L.: Art and Collaboration', National Gallery of Art, Washington, D.C., November 15, 1984–February 24, 1985.

1985

'David Hockney (Photocollages)/Roland Reiss', Elaine Horwitch Galleries, Scottsdale, Arizona, January 3–29. 'Representation Abroad – Diversity', Hirshhorn Museum and Sculpture Garden, Washington, D.C., June 6–September 2. 'Automobile and Culture – Detroit Style', Detroit Institute of Art, Detroit, Michigan, June 9–September 10. Paris Biennale, Paris, March–May. 'Anniversary Exhibition of 150 Selected Prints', Associated American Artists, New York, March. 'Paperworks from Tyler Graphics', Walker Art Center, Minneapolis, April 13–June 16. 'Drawings: Coast to Coast', Gallery One, Fort Worth, Texas, April 27–June 1. 'Summer Group Show', L.A. Louver Gallery, Venice, California, July 16–August 17. 'A–Z: Works on Paper', Bernard Jacobson Gallery, Los Angeles, June–July. 'A Second Talent: Painters and Sculptors who are also Photographers'. The Aldrich Museum of Contemporary Art, Ridgefield, Connecticut, September 22–December 15. 'The Painter's Music/The Musician's Art'. A Collaboration with the An Die Musik Chamber Ensemble, Helen Frankenthaler, David Hockney, Robert Motherwell, Kenneth Noland, Solomon R. Guggenheim Museum, November 17.

1986

'Master Drawings from The Drawing Society's Membership', New York, February 12–March 8. 'Music and the Visual Arts in the 20th Century', Palais de Beaux-Arts, Brussels, February 22–April 6. 'Photomosaics: The Landscape Reconstructed', Photographic Resource Center, Boston University, Boston, Mass., February 27–April 4. 'Painters in the Theatre in the 20 Century', Frankfurt, February 28–May 19. Adelaide Festival of Photography, Adelaide, March 3–23. 'Works by Contemporary Masters', Thomas Babeor Gallery, La Jolla, California, March 7–May 3. 'Drawing: A Classical Continuum', Los Angeles Municipal Art Gallery, Los Angeles, March 18–April 13. 'Self-Portraits by Clemente, Kelly and Hockney', Blum Helman Gallery, New York, March 5–29. 'The Real Big Picture', The Queen's Museum, Queens, New York. January 17–March 19. 'Portraits', Martina Hamilton Gallery, New York, April 18–May 3. 'Master Drawings 1918–1985', Janie C. Lee Gallery, New York, March. 'Major New Works', Richard Gray Gallery, Chicago, Illinois, May. 'Structured Vision: Collaged and Sequential Photography', The Boise Gallery of Art, Boise, Idaho, November 21 1986–February 1988, travelling to: Whatcom Museum, Bellingham, Washington; Fort Wayne Museum of Art, Fort Wayne, Indiana; Cheney Cowles Memorial Museum, Spokane, Washington; Sonoma State University, Sonoma, California; and University of Oklahoma, Norman, Oklahoma. 'Summer 1986, Selected Works', Thomas Babeor Gallery, La Jolla, California, August 1–30. 'Pavilion at the Ideal Home', Arts Council of Great Britain, London, Summer. 'Contemporary Screens: Function, Decoration, Sculpture, Metaphor', Art Museum Association organized two-year travelling tour to the following cities: Contemporary Arts Center, Cincinnati; The Wright Art Gallery, Los Angeles; The Lowe Art Museum, Coral Gables, Florida; The Toledo Art Museum, Toledo, Ohio; Desmoines Art Center, Desmoines, Iowa; Lakeview Museum of Arts and Sciences; Raleigh Center for Contemporary Art, September 1986–1988. 'The Artist in the Theatre', Kunsthalle, Frankfurt, February 28–May 19. 'Poetics of Space', Museum of Fine Arts, Museum of New Mexico, Santa Fe, New Mexico, December 19, 1986–March 22, 1987. 'Interaction: Art-Music-Art'. Camden Arts Centre, London, November 12–December 21.

1987

'Modern and Contemporary Masters', Richard Gray Gallery, Chicago, Illinois, January 31–March 7. 'Artists by Artists: Portrait Photographs from Art News, 1904–1986', International Center of Photography, New York, February 27–April 19. 'Contemporary Los Angeles', Taipei Fine Arts Museum, Taipei, Taiwan, April 4–June 10. 'Berlin Art 1961–1987', Museum of Modern Art, New York, May 27–September 8. 'Word & Image', Holman Hall Art Gallery, Trenton State College, April–May. 'The Artist's Mother: Portraits and Homages', Heckscher Museum, Huntington, New York, November 1987–January 1988, travels to The National Portrait Gallery, London, April 1987–May 1988. 'The World Is Round: The Artist and the Expansive Vision', Hudson River Museum, Yonkers, New York, November 1987–February 1989, travels to Delaware Art Museum, Wilmington; Parrish Art Museum, Southampton; Arts & Science Center, Nashua, N.H.; Albany Institute of History & Art; College Art Gallery, New Paltz. 'Contemporary American Stage Design', Milwaukee Art Museum, Milwaukee, September–November. 'Legacy of Light', International Center of Photography, New York, November 1987–January 1988. Book published by Alfred A. Knopf, exhibition of photographs in book. 'British Art in the Twentieth Century: The Modern Movement', Royal Academy of Arts, London, January–April. 'Group Show' (De Kooning, Kline, Hockney, Diebenkorn, Motherwell, Hofmann), Thomas Babeor Gallery, La Jolla, California, Summer. 'Contemporary Los Angeles', Amerika Haus, Berlin, July. 'Pop Art: USA-UK'. Odakyu Grand Gallery, Tokyo, July–August; Daimaru Museum, Osaka, September; Funabashi Seibu Museum of Art, Funabashi, October–November; Sogo Museum of Art, Yokohama, November–December. 'Twenty Artists + Twenty Techniques', Albemarle Gallery, London, July 8–August 7. 'The Artists of California: A Group Portrait in Mixed Media', Oakland Museum, California, July 14, 1987–January 10, 1988; travels to Crocker Art Museum, Sacramento; Laguna Art Museum, Laguna. 'Ten British Masters', Arnold Herstand & Co., New York, October 23–December 5. 'A Collection Revisited', The Chrysler Museum, Norfolk, Virginia, September.

1988

'First Person Singular: Self-Portrait Photography 1840–1986', High Museum, Atlanta, Georgia, January 7–March 14. 'The British Picture', L.A. Louver Gallery, Venice, California, February 5–April 9. 'Perspective on 20th Century Paintings', Nagoya City Art Museum, Nagoya, Japan, April 23–June 19.

Photographic Work by Paul Joyce

1974 Photographs included in 'New Photography' at the Midland Group Gallery, Nottingham.   *1976* Victoria and Albert Museum acquire a portfolio of photographs.   *1977* First one-man show at the Photographic Gallery, Southampton. Work included in 'Summer Show' at the Serpentine Gallery, Hyde Park, and 'Singular Realities' at the Side Gallery, Newcastle. Portfolios of photographs acquired by the Arts Council and the Department of the Environment.   *1978* One-man show, 'Elders', at the National Portrait Gallery, London. Exhibition of landscape photographs opens at the Diaframma Gallery, Milan, then tours Italy sponsored by the British Council.   *1979* Exhibits at the Cultural Section of SICOF in Milan. Work included in 'Nine Contemporary Photographers' at the Witkin Gallery, New York, and 'The Native Land' in Llandudno and Bristol.   *1980* Major photographic retrospective opens at the Photographic Gallery, Cardiff, then tours Wales. Exhibits at British Group Show, Sydney.   *1981* Work included in 'British Art 1940–1980' at the Hayward Gallery, London. Exhibits at the Bibliothèque Nationale, Paris, which then acquires a major portfolio of work.   *1982* One-man show at Contrasts Gallery, London. Work included in 'The Photographer as Printmaker' at the Photographer's Gallery, London.   *1984* First book of photographs, *From Edge to Edge*, a monograph of Welsh landscapes, published. One-man shows at the Pentonville Gallery, London, and the Pentax Forum, Tokyo.   *1985* Abandons photography as a result of a growing disenchantment with the medium.   *1987* Retrospectives of his film work at the Rotterdam Film Festival and Salso Film Festival, Rome.

Picture Credits

Bibliography

Berman, Morris, *Re-enchantment of the World*, Cornell University Press, New York, 1982

Brandt, Bill, *Literary Britain*, Victoria & Albert Museum, London, 1984

Cartier-Bresson, Henri, *The Decisive Moment*, Viking Press, New York

Edgerton, Samuel, *The Renaissance Rediscovery of Linear Perspective*, Harper & Row, New York, 1975

Ferguson, Marilyn, *The Aquarian Conspiracy*, Routledge, London, 1981

Gombrich, Ernst, *Art and Illusion*, Phaidon, Oxford, 1977

Guillen, Michael, *Bridges to Infinity – The Human Side to Mathematics*, Jeremy P. Tarcher, Inc. Publisher, Los Angeles, 1983

Hockney, David, *Six Fairy Tales of the Brothers Grimm* (David Hockney) 1969

——*72 Drawings by David Hockney*, Jonathan Cape, London, and Viking, New York, 1971

——*David Hockney by David Hockney*, Thames and Hudson, London, 1976

——*Blue Guitar*, Petersburg Press, London, 1977

——*Travels with Pen, Pencil and Ink*, Petersburg Press, London, 1978

——*Pictures*, Thames and Hudson, London, 1979

——*David Hockney Prints 1954–77*, Scottish Arts Council, Edinburgh, 1979

——*Paper Pools*, Thames and Hudson, London, 1980

——*Looking at Pictures in a Book*, Petersburg Press, London, 1981

——*Photographs*, Petersburg Press, London, 1982

——*Hockney Paints the Stage*, Abbeville Press, New York, 1983

——*Martha's Vineyard and Other Places*, Thames and Hudson, London, 1985

——*On Photography*, André Emmerich, New York, 1983: reprinted Bradford 1985

——*Vogue*, French Vogue, Paris, December 1985

——*Home Made Prints by David Hockney* (David Hockney) 1986

——*Hockney Posters*, Pavilion Books, London, 1987

——*Faces*, Thames and Hudson, London, 1987

——*David Hockney: A Retrospective*, Thames and Hudson, London, 1987

Jaynes, Julian, *The Origin of Consciousness in the Breakdown of the Bicameral Mind*, Penguin, Harmondsworth, 1982

Joyce, Paul, *From Edge to Edge*, Lucida Publications, London, 1983

Leshan, L. N. and Margenau, Henry, *Einstein's Space and Van Gogh's Sky*, Harvester Press, Brighton, 1983

Panofsky, Erwin, 'Die Perspektiv als "symbolische Form"', Hamburg, 1927

Rowley, George, *Principles of Chinese Painting*, Princeton University Press, 1959

Rubin, William S., *Pablo Picasso: A Retrospective*, Thames and Hudson, London, 1980

Sontag, Susan, *On Photography*, Penguin, Harmondsworth, 1979

Spender, Stephen, *Citizens in War – and After*, Harrap, London, 1945

——and Hockney, David, *China Diary*, Thames and Hudson, London, 1982

Steinberg, Leo, *Other Criteria*, Oxford University Press, 1975

Weschler, Lawrence, *Cameraworks – David Hockney*, Thames and Hudson, London, 1984

Zukav, Gary, *The Dancing Wu Li Masters*, Fontana, London, 1984

Index